The Small Business Start-Up Guide

A *Surefire* Blueprint to *Successfully* Launch Your Own Business

MATTHEW THOMPSON & MICHAEL GIABRONE

5TH EDITION

 SO

Published by Sourcebooks, Inc.
P.O. Box 4410, Naperville, Illinois 60567-4410
(630) 961-3900
Fax: (630) 961-2168
www.sourcebooks.com

Thompson, Matthew (Business writer)
  The small business start-up guide : a surefire blueprint to successfully launch your own business / by Matthew Thompson and Michael Giabrone.—Fifth edition.
       pages cm
  Revision of: The small business start-up guide / Hal Root and Steve Koenig.
  Includes index.
  1. New business enterprises—United States—Handbooks, manuals, etc. I. Giabrone, Michael. II. Root, Hal, Small business start-up guide. III. Title.
  HD62.5.R66 2013
  658.1'1--dc23
                              2012046646

Printed and bound in the United States of America.

VP 10 9 8 7 6 5 4 3 2 1

Contents

Contents

Introduction

Small business is the backbone of the American economy. In a sense, it always has been. From the first shopkeepers of the thirteen colonies to the local restaurateurs of today, small business has been the one constant economic force in America. Today, fully one-half of all workers in the private sector are employed by the nation's twenty-nine million small businesses.

Since you've picked up this book, it's likely that you are one of the millions of Americans employed by a large company, the government, or an agriculture or a nonprofit organization, or you are unemployed and looking for a change. Whatever your reason or current employment situation, you have decided to purchase this book—and by doing so, you have decided to join the small business economic juggernaut. Maybe your business will be part-time and home based. Maybe you will decide to chuck it all and go full-time, sinking all your time and money into it. Whatever you decide, you have picked our book to help guide you through the start-up, and we will do just that.

The Small Business Start-Up Guide is a fact-filled account of the dos and don'ts of starting a small business in the twenty-first century. The pertinent information is presented without the clutter of gregarious psychological booster material. You can get that somewhere else. However, it is necessary to be serious and excited about your proposed business, which is why we wrote this book in a style that is easy to follow and quick to read.

Although this book is intended for a beginner, an established businessperson also can use it as a reference guide or, better yet, give it to another potential entrepreneur to read. The more people who know the basic facts about starting a business, the better.

What Is a Small Business?

The first eye-opening fact about small business is that there's really not much that's small about it at all. Let's start with the basics: according to the latest figures from the U.S. Small Business Administration, a small business is any independent company that employs fewer than five hundred workers. But small businesses also

- Represent 99.7 percent of all employer firms
- Employ about half of all private-sector employees
- Pay 43 percent of the total U.S. private payroll

- Have generated 65 percent of net new jobs over the past seventeen years
- Create more than half of the nonfarm private gross domestic product
- Hire 43 percent of high-tech workers (scientists, engineers, computer programmers, and others)
- Are 52 percent home based and 2 percent franchises
- Made up 97.5 percent of all identified exporters and produced 31 percent of export value in the 2008 fiscal year
- Produce 16.5 times more patents per employee than large patenting firms

These might be statistics worth remembering when you start thinking you're too "small" to compete.

You're considering this option at a fascinating time. The U.S. Census Bureau reported in May 2012 that U.S. business start-ups have been declining since the 1980s, and the number of new small businesses dropped sharply during the 2008–2009 recession. Does that mean the United States has become less entrepreneurial or more risk averse?

That's a question for the historians. This book is about you.

On the ground, depending on your ideas and business focus, less competition and more fear among the competition might be a very good thing. First, the advantages and risks involved in starting a small business are not lost on you because you have made the first crucial decision: to go through the processes of starting a successful one. You're starting the important work right now. Second, the time is right for smart, risk-taking businesspeople to take control of the market. Despite the shaky economy, in some ways there has never been a better time to start a small business.

A Word about Small Office and Home Office Businesses

Small office and home office (SOHO) businesses—some call the operators of these businesses "homepreneurs"—are ever-increasing parts of the small business mix, and a part you should consider, at least at the start.

Home-based businesses now represent half of all the U.S.-based companies that fit the U.S. Small Business Administration's definition of small business. That means that roughly fifteen million businesses have been formed and are being run by individuals in their homes. Many of these are referred to as microbusinesses, which are companies that have one or two employees overall.

Technology is a huge driver behind the growth of businesses like these. Besides a work space, basic computer and Internet connectivity, and a phone, not much else is needed for most nonmanufacturing businesses to start these days. Even the financial investment in computing has become considerably smaller than it was a decade ago. First, there's what's happening on the hardware side. The actual machinery of computing—the computers themselves, monitors, and printers—is moving from desktop to handheld devices. And on the software side, traditional store-bought software CDs are moving toward cloud-based computing (where you essentially log on to a site on the Internet to access the programs you need and don't need to buy physical software at all). Finally, the work itself is moving into a more collaborative, virtual environment thanks to software that more than several people can use at the same time.

In the future, you might be running your business solely from a smartphone or tablet computer. And who knows? The traditional office may be going the way of the dodo.

What This Book Offers

This book provides a walk-through of all the steps to get a business up and running, from visualization to financing to actual start-up. It also provides invaluable back-of-the-book resources that will help you jump-start your business from home or from a commercial space. We really think you're going to like our new resource sections.

Since the last edition of this book was published, we've seen an incredible evolution in how state and local governments handle business information on the Internet. In chapter 14, which features our state-by-state guide to business registration guidelines and forms, we now give you shortcuts to the main locations of up-to-the-minute resources for governmental business registration, tax and labor information on the web, as well as contact information for phone and traditional mail.

Why? Because laws, regulations, and, most important, form and document names and filing numbers change within state and local governments on a daily basis anywhere in the country—from the moment the book you hold in your hands is published. So in this edition we're providing you multiple ways to contact agencies so you can have greater speed and accuracy in tracking down forms and answering questions.

But that's not all we've changed in chapter 14. Starting a business is a holistic endeavor that involves legal, tax, and financial planning for both home and business. So we're supplying a wider variety of resources to help you find the best attorneys, certified public accountants, and financial planners in your community.

Three appendixes conclude the book. Appendix A lists the Small Business Administration's publications, which may be helpful to you at various stages of your business start-up. Appendix B shares a table of state tax rates. Appendix C contains all the worksheets provided within the book, plus a few extra, for handy photocopying and easy use.

The Usual Disclaimers

As we will state often, this book should in no way be considered a legal guide. *Never* take legal advice from anyone but a lawyer. However, the information contained herein is factual and researched. Any omissions or errors are purely unintentional. The authors assume no responsibility for misinterpretation, unintentional error, or misprints. This is a guide to use along with the professional and legal help you seek. It is a very informative overview designed to get you thinking about the pitfalls and possibilities ahead.

Why We Wrote This Book

By recognizing the pros and cons of starting a small business, you will be better able to deal with the complexities of running your business later. We say this because in March 2002, we incorporated our own small business. The process was filled with headaches, technicalities, and little problems that became large ones. The entire process, from seeing a lawyer to getting the last document we needed, was an incredibly stressful and confusing two and a half months. Some of this was a result of unnecessary bureaucracy, but most was because of our own ignorance of the proper procedures and requirements.

What we would have given for a straightforward, concise guide to incorporation and starting up a business. We needed not motivation or books describing trends in businesses but solid information without all the accompanying fluff. Unfortunately, all we found at the local bookstores were motivational and trendy books. While those books might have been relevant to some people, to us they were simply impediments to finding the information we needed. The solid how-to information on starting a business was elusive, so we decided that we would share with you the things we found out firsthand—the hard way.

On the personal side, we would like to thank the staff at Sourcebooks for help and counsel. Particular thanks go to Dominique Raccah, the publisher who first gave this book a chance, and to Peter Lynch.

We hope *The Small Business Start-Up Guide* is useful in the formation of your small business, whatever its size. Wishing you luck, success, and profits!

—Matthew Thompson and Michael Giabrone

March 2013

Chapter

1

Are You Really Ready to Start Your Own Business? Questions to Ask Yourself at Start-Up

By purchasing this book, you've decided to take control of your future in a way many fear to do. That said, the time for procrastination is over. You have decided that your business idea is feasible and that you will begin the process of testing your business concept and starting it. We think that's great.

But before you actually proceed with the start-up procedures, you should take some time to prepare yourself for what will happen after you begin the process of establishing a small business. Your life is going to change substantially. Starting a business doesn't just mean you're doing something different during working hours. You're going to be making decisions that affect not only you but also your family and others you involve in this new enterprise. And this venture won't just concern business finances. It will affect your personal finances, too.

But here's the good news: You get to decide what the outcome of your investment will be. You get to set specific goals on what you want your company to be and to accomplish. You get to consider how happy you want to be at work and how much money you want or need to earn to stay happy. Most important—and particularly relevant for those who will remember the worst economic downturn since the Great Depression—you alone will set the goals for your business and make the decision to grow, sell, or end the business on the basis of its progress.

It's all in your hands.

While this book is devoted to starting, rather than running, a small business, we feel that now—in the beginning—is the time to ask vital questions about yourself, your goals, and your business idea in general. Maybe you have already done that; maybe you have asked every imaginable question of yourself and your business. That's good. But chances are you have not asked enough questions. No one can ever question or research a business idea enough.

You also have to be innovative enough to look ahead. For instance, in 1975 there was no personal computer market, but a handful of innovators and forward-thinking computer enthusiasts believed that people would eventually want a computer in their homes. The result— well, you know the result. Had those people decided that there was no market for personal computing, scores of firms would not exist. Nothing is disingenuous or wrong about starting a business in uncharted territory or with lingering questions. But by asking questions, thinking about them, and researching the answers, you can highlight and eliminate many problem areas before you start. Then, while you're running your business, you can tackle the lingering questions—and hopefully come up with answers as successful as Microsoft's and IBM's were.

It is sheer suicide to go into business without being motivated or prepared for the responsibilities. Believe it or not, being motivated does not mean not having doubts. Everyone has doubts, even successful entrepreneurs. It's human nature. Rather, proper motivation means confronting and conquering your doubts before turning to the fulfillment of your dreams. Your motivation has to last before, during, and after you start your business. If you can accomplish this, you will be on your way to success, rather than being one of the thousands of businesses that fail or go bankrupt each year. That is, you must have an underlying desire, need, or want in order to keep the fire of your dream alive, especially during the lean start-up times.

Whatever your motivation—you hate the boss at your corporate job, you have a great product or skill, or you just want to work for yourself—now is the time to solidify that motivation by questioning it.

Am I Ready for Self-Employment?

Right now, you're likely in that enthusiastic stage of any new enterprise—the planning stages, before you've actually pulled the trigger. You're starting to envision yourself in a completely new role, executing a new idea you've honed for a while and calling the shots. In the best case, this is what starting a business really does feel like. Confidence, enthusiasm, and excitement are all key to this process.

But if you've spent your working life up until now employed by others, your lifestyle is going to change considerably in terms of hours, your relationship to money, and even your relationships with those close to you. You'll never have a full picture of what these changes might be until you go through them, but we can provide some general ideas:

• **Workday changes:** Most start-ups begin with the founder at the helm for every hour that business is open, and that usually means every hour until the work gets done to meet proper deadlines or goals. But with most new businesses, we're not talking about the conventional eight-hour day you might have worked for others. If you're operating a store, your business might have regular hours. But once the doors are locked and the lights are off, your workday very likely won't be at an end. You might be washing the floors, restocking the shelves, and doing what's required as to daily bookkeeping and cash management. Even desktop-based businesses have these beginning or end-of-day support activities that require you to evaluate the day and plan for the next one. You will discover very quickly that time management is one of the most important things you must master in working for yourself, or else you will be working all the time.

QUICK Tip

Time Management: The best way to understand time management in your future business is to study similar successful businesses and how their owners manage their time. Learn to ask very specific questions about how competing owners plan their day, what they do during working hours, and how they prepare for the upcoming day, week, and month.

- **Money changes:** The question of money and self-employment is one of the most complicated you'll face, and it's best you consider it now in the start-up phase, preferably while you're still getting a weekly paycheck from someone else. To use the most simplistic example, the money considerations of a business go far beyond what you'll need to have in the cash register every day in order to make change for your customers. Addressing the financial issues of a business involves determining whether you're covering the basic costs of space, utilities, and payroll and achieving a target profit to stay in business. But there's another dimension of planning the money issues for a business, and it's one that many fledgling entrepreneurs forget in the rush to try their ideas: planning the money issues for themselves and their personal lives. Do you know what amount of money you'll need to make to pay for your personal and your family's critical expenses? Will you be able to stretch your new salary to pay for a home, afford medical insurance, and eventually send your kids to college? Planning financially for a business should be a parallel process—planning financially for the business and planning financially for yourself and the lives of those you love.

QUICK Tip

Getting Advice: Parallel planning for the money needs of a business should start not with the business, but what you'll need to make to support you and your family. It is wise to consult a trained financial planning professional before you take on the risk of a business because it is critical to examine your current income stream, your household expenses, the cost of your healthcare, personal insurance, and other key benefits and necessities to determine how much money you'll have to make in business to sustain your current lifestyle. A good resource is the Financial Planning Association's PlannerSearch page at www.fpanet.org. You'll find planners in your area with specific expertise in working with independent businesspeople.

- **Lifestyle changes:** Those of us who work long hours in our businesses should be doing it because we love it and because those close to us support what we're doing. Starting a small business requires you to work long hours planning it, operating it during business hours, and often spending after-work hours thinking about the business and planning future strategies. Are you ready for that? Are your family and friends ready for that? It's a critical issue you need to explore before you make the commitment.

Do I Have the Serious Motivation to Succeed?

Being a modern American small businessperson is not easy. You need flexibility and determination to become a successful businessperson in today's high-pressure, highly competitive small business world. All companies, regardless of size, must change and adapt to the environment and current trends in order to survive and flourish. Staying put does not win the race. Can you, as a small businessperson, change and accept new ideas or methods in order to keep or gain market share?

Initially, you will have a hectic and possibly frustrating time starting your small business. After all, you have to sell your product or service, deliver it to your customers' satisfaction, and maintain the momentum of your start-up. Then come more twelve- to fourteen-hour workdays, seven-day workweeks, and self-sacrifices that must be endured for

QUICK Tip

Transitioning into Business Ownership: This is not possible for every type of business, but it might make sense to keep working at your current job while planning and eventually starting up your company. As mentioned in the previous section on money changes, some financial advisers encourage this because many businesses take weeks, months, or possibly years to start turning an operating profit, and until then, you'll still have to make sure you've got enough money for basic living expenses. But there's another important reason to try this beyond the financial issues—you'll get an early idea of whether you actually want to be in business before you take on the full financial risk.

whatever period of time it takes for you to be successful. And once "there"—wherever it is your goals take you—you must continually strive for better and more success. This is what staying power is all about. Those who can change and adapt and work hard at it will be successful. Those who can't will probably end up working for others their whole lives.

Am I Prepared to Compete?

Small business failure statistics are nothing new, but given the economic downturn that began in 2007, entrepreneurs have had to learn new lessons in order to keep themselves afloat. You'll have the benefit of starting a new enterprise after the worst economic downturn in seventy years, but as this book was being published, the economy wasn't out of the woods yet.

In a February 2012 report, Dun & Bradstreet reported that the smallest of small companies—those with fewer than fifty employees—were still struggling. From 2008 to 2011, the number of bankruptcies dropped by 2.5 percent for businesses with 50 to 99 employees, by 17 percent for businesses with 100 to 499 employees, and by 50 percent for large businesses with more than 500 employees. However, the number of bankruptcies increased by 10 percent for businesses in the smallest size class over that time period. According to D&B, "The recovery of businesses from the recession seems to be related to their size class, with

Getting Your Share: Determining your potential market share is crucial. When developing your business plan (see chapter 4 and Appendix C), be sure to determine the maturity of your product or service within your industry and the potential economic and social trends that might affect its success.

the lower size classes recovering more gradually and the lowest size class still reeling in its wake" ("Delinquency and Failure by Industry," U.S. Business Trends Report, February 2012).

What should that tell you? The smallest competitors are the most vulnerable. Knowing the odds before beginning a business and then developing a plan to beat those odds is one way to remain competitive.

As we have mentioned already, hard work and persistence are important. But so are other things such as timing, initiative, pricing, product, marketing, the economy, and even luck. These same criteria affect every business in America, though not always in the same ways. Businesses that fail can fail for many reasons.

Since so many people are starting businesses, especially small office and home office (SOHO) businesses, your competition is fierce. While not all other small businesses will be your direct competitors, the proliferation of small businesses means that more parties are going after a finite number of consumer dollars. You have to compete for those dollars. In some industries, you'll be dealing with free-trade laws that give foreign companies greater access to American markets. In all industries, you'll be up against other small businesses with more start-up capital, as well as experienced competitors already plying their trade. And in all cases, you'll be up against smarter, better-informed people.

In short, you're up against a lot, but the rewards of success are very sweet, and with all of the help and assistance available to today's small business owner, you're well ahead of your predecessors from ten or twenty years ago. Ultimately, for you to succeed, you have to take on those hundreds of thousands of other people like you who are starting their own businesses—and beat them. You have to win. Why? Because that's the only way to realize your dream.

Think Ahead: Any set of factors can adversely affect a small business: a failing economy; a poor marketing scheme; a poor product or service; a saturated marketplace; and lack of financing, experience, or desire. Even personal problems such as a divorce or poor health threaten your business's survival.

The answer to the question of whether you are ready to compete should reveal whether it is time for you to really think about your business structure. After all, your small business undoubtedly will be a learning experience, but it need not be traumatic, as long as you plan your course and confront your obstacles. You can't know everything up front, but confronting the important issues ahead of time will be a great benefit.

The Complete Start-Up Questions

The next set of questions involve who, what, where, why, when, and how. As you answer these questions, you will begin to see how much or how little you know about your potential business. If your answers disappoint you, take corrective actions. Research the answers through creative methods and resources. Find out what you need to do if you don't know how to answer a question. Find the solutions before you go any farther.

These questions, as well as your own that you will think up, are good starting points for beginning a business. There is no real order to these questions. Just ask and answer them in any order you like. You can think over or skip questions that don't exactly pertain to you.

Who?
1. Who are my potential employees?
    • Do I need any?
    • What skills should I look for in employees?
    • How will I get them and which resources will I use (e.g., temp agencies, want ads)?
    • What is the demographic composition of the local labor force?

2. Who are my potential customers?
   - How can I ensure that customers are attracted and stay attracted to my service or product?
   - How will I get these customers in the first place?
   - Is my customer base general or specific in nature?
   - How do I reach them? What kind of advertising or online communication should I do?
3. Who are my competitors?
   - How will I compete with them on price, quality, service, and location?
   - Are they too competitive or too entrenched?
   - Are they successful?
   - What are their weaknesses?
   - Is the market oversaturated?
4. Who will be my investors, partner(s), or company officers?
   - Do I need partners?
   - Do I work better alone? Can I work alone?
   - How do I pick a partner?
   - Should I have general or limited partners?
   - Will they be committed to the business?
   - Will I make a supreme effort to make good use of investors' capital?
   - Will I involve friends or family as investors, and how should I handle their involvement?

What?

1. What is my product or service?
   - Have I sold, made, or offered these products or services in the past?
   - How am I different? How will I differentiate my service or product?
   - Is it different, unique, or better than the competition?
   - How will I pick supply and service vendors?
   - Is there a market for these services or products?
   - How do I fulfill customers' orders or requests? What is my distribution channel?
   - Do I have confidence that what I am making, providing, or selling is of good quality?
   - Can I sell my product or service online?
2. What compensation do I offer any employees I may have?
   - Do I take a salary?
   - Do I know how to do payroll?

- How many employees can I afford at different salaries?
- Can I attract quality employees with the wages I can offer?
- Can I use nonpay incentives like comp time or stock options?
- Do I know what competitors are paying employees?
- Should I combine pay with bonuses?

3. What benefits can I offer?
- Should I provide benefits to myself or to my employees?
- What, if any, benefits can I afford?
- Are there associations or small business co-ops that share group benefits? If so, what are they?
- Regardless of employees, do I personally need vacation time, health coverage, or a pension?

4. What sources of help are available to me?
- Can my local or state government offer start-up assistance?
- What start-up resources does the Small Business Administration offer?
- What magazines, radio and television programs, private companies, and national small business organizations are available to me?

Where?

1. Where will I buy or lease an office, store, warehouse, or plant?
- Do I really need a commercial space to operate my business?
- Can I start with a home office?
- Can I meet zoning requirements at home?
- How much space do I need?
- What office and computer equipment do I need?
- Can I work at home with no interruptions?
- Will I need a separate phone line? A post office box? An answering service?
- Can I really afford the space I'm going to need?

2. Where will I get start-up funding?
- Can I obtain a loan at a bank or credit union? Will the institution loan money for a start-up business?
- What kind of shape is my credit in?
- Do the institutions I have in mind lend to SOHO businesses?
- Am I willing to use my savings and investments?
- Will family and friends invest with me?
- Can I get development capital from the Small Business Administration or other state and local government entities?

- Do I qualify for minority- or women-owned business loans, programs, and/or grants?
- Should I try to get funding from an angel investor or a venture capitalist?

3. Where do I want to be (in life) in five, ten, fifteen, and twenty years? (This is a personal as well as a business question. Answer it and the following questions for yourself and your business.)

- What are my short-term goals?
- What are my long-term goals?
- Are my ultimate goals financial or based on satisfaction?
- How will my business goals adversely affect my family life?
- Are my goals realistic?
- How will I evaluate my success?
- If I do not achieve my goals, what will I do?

Why?

1. Why should I choose a sole proprietorship, partnership, limited liability company, or corporation? (Also, what are the advantages and disadvantages of each?)

- How big do I need to be to start out?
- Which aspects of each entity appeal to me?
- Which state, local government, tax, regulatory, and/or licensing issues will affect my choice of entity?
- Do I need to consider the liability protection offered by a corporation or limited liability company?

2. Why should I go into business in the first place?

- What are my real reasons and motivations? Are they personal, professional, or other?
- Are my reasons supportable? Am I doing this for positive rather than negative reasons?
- Do I want to make a lot of money? Or am I in it for the potential freedom that owning a business can offer?

When?

1. When should I start my business?

- Will the economy—local, regional, state, national—support my idea?
- Should I continue to work in my current job while starting the business?

- Is my business a growth industry?
- Am I starting my business at the right time to take advantage of the market?

2. When will I find time for family and friends? (We have restated this point for emphasis.)
- Can I afford the social costs of starting a business?
- Is it possible to let family and friends work with me in the business?
- Am I prepared for the loneliness of going it alone?

How?

3. How will I promote my business and/or product or service?
- What percentage of promotion can I do online (e.g., website, social media, blogging) versus other, more expensive forms of advertising?
- Can I get free publicity?
- Can I sponsor teams, programs, or events?
- Would conventional advertising in the Yellow Pages, print magazine, or newspaper benefit my business?
- How can networking at small business organizations and the local chamber of commerce help me?

4. How much start-up capital will I need?
- What are my initial fixed costs?
- What will be my eventual fixed and variable costs?
- Can I get assistance to determine my start-up needs?
- How do I manage my business?
- How are payroll, accounting, human resource management, regulatory paperwork, tax filing, billing, and communication done in my chosen business arena? Do I know how to do all of these, especially if I have a SOHO business?
- Do I know an accountant, lawyer, or SCORE officer (an employee of a non-profit business mentoring organization) who can help me plan for these eventualities?
- What computer software will be most helpful to me?

Hopefully, you have been able to answer many of these questions, and hopefully you have come up with dozens of others specifically related to your situation and business. A worksheet is included in figure 1.1 for you jot down questions and answers. Bookmark the page so you can note them as you read.

Gathering questions and answering as many as you can is the most vital thing you can do at this stage. No one goes into business thinking he or she has all the answers.

As noted, you can ask and answer these questions to help shape your initial business plan and influence your start-up operations. Chapter 3 explores research and start-up planning and contains useful information on how to find answers to many of the questions you will ask. You will then use those answers as foundations to the various parts of your business plan, explained in chapter 4, where you will learn how all the information you gathered can be integrated into your business plan.

No doubt you might have some lingering questions that seem to defy answers. That's OK. As long as you honestly answer the bulk of your important questions, you will be in a great position to move ahead. You will have answers and rock-solid self-motivation, which should be a driving force behind your business start-up. Proper motivation ensures that you will stick to your plans with the discipline necessary in running a small business.

QUICK Tip

Use the SBA Website: The U.S. Small Business Administration offers a list of frequently asked questions for the potential businessperson; you might want to start there to build your foundation of start-up skills. It's an excellent resource to use in combination with this chapter. The address is http://www.sbaonline.sba.gov.

Figure 1.1: QUESTIONS AND ANSWERS WORKSHEET

Use this worksheet to jot down questions you have about
the process of starting a business. The sources provided
in this book should help you answer almost any question
you come up with.

Q. _____
_____
_____

A. _____
_____
_____

Q. _____
_____
_____

A. _____
_____
_____

Q. _____
_____
_____

A. _____
_____
_____

Q. _____
_____
_____

A. _____
_____
_____

Chapter 2

The Nine Great Steps to Start-Up Success

▶ **Determine your product or service**

▶ **Research your idea**

▶ **Make the Internet work for you**

▶ **Develop a business plan**

▶ **Consult a lawyer, an accountant, and a financial planner**

▶ **Determine your business entity**

▶ **Seek government help**

▶ **Start your business**

▶ **Seek sources of financing**

After you get the itch to start a business, the cycle begins to take on a life of its own. After you decide that you have a product or service that will appeal to a segment of the market and that you have the determination to do it right, you have to begin the start-up process. That process includes researching your idea, writing a business plan, filing forms, obtaining licenses, and—finally—conducting business. By following the guidance in this book, you can eliminate uncertainty about which steps to take and concentrate on being as effective in your start-up practices as you can be. If your start-up is successful, it will impart that much more confidence as you continue. A bad experience in the beginning can taint your whole operation.

The process of starting a small business, from idea to entity, can be broken down into a series of stages or steps. In this chapter, we have broken down the process into the following nine easy steps that you can use as a guideline. The idea is to follow each step in order, thus staying organized and eliminating possible confusion. Each step pushes the process forward until you are actually in business.

The Nine Great Steps

Although no two start-ups are the same, most will follow an underlying set course. This chapter describes such a course. This nine-step process is generic in nature and meant to cover every type of start-up, from sole proprietors to corporations. Obviously, some of the steps will not have the same bearing on certain entities as they will on others. For instance, a corporation will probably require a much more extensive business plan than a simple sole proprietorship. Conversely, a sole proprietor may not necessarily need to consult a lawyer or an accountant. The key to this guide is to use it as a flexible, all-purpose list. If one step does not pertain to you, skip it and move on to the next one.

Step 1: Determine Your Product or Service

This step is when you will determine which product or service you have decided to offer consumers. Even if you have already made this choice, now is the time to hone the idea and shape its actual identity.

If your business will be a service, define which exact services you will offer and how. For instance, if you open an accounting firm, you need to define which services you will offer: general services for the

Figure 2.1: **THE NINE GREAT STEPS**

The nine great steps to launching a successful business are as follows:

1. Determine your product or service.
2. Research your idea.
3. Make the Internet work for you.
4. Develop a business plan.
5. Consult a lawyer, an accountant, and a financial planner.
6. Determine your business entity.
7. Seek government help.
8. Start your business.
9. Seek sources of financing.

whole market or specific services for market niches like tax accounting or business accounting. If you decide to open a clothing store, you must decide which type of clothing you will sell. You have to decide where you will sell it and how you will obtain the clothes for resale. In short, prepare an organized outline of every part of the service (this is different from the business plan, discussed later). Know what you are going to provide and how you plan on providing it.

If your business is product driven, you must do one of two things. Write a product prospectus and make a model of it, or contract a company to make a model, so that you and others see what it is that you are making. Either way, you must have a physical sample of your product and a statement of what it will do.

QUICK Tip

Describe Your Product: A product prospectus is simply a short report on your product—how it is made, how it can be used, and how it is better than similar existing products. If it is a unique or new product, you might have to obtain a patent or trademark.

Time Frame: Product and service generation and research may take weeks, months, or even years, but it is a crucial step. If you are developing a product, make sure you offer the best you can; it may take more time, but it will be financially well worth it.

Step 2: Research Your Idea

You can never have too much information, especially in the competitive world of small business. This vital step of research is intended to allow you to sharpen your knowledge of business and your chosen field. While you are honing your idea, go to anyone and everyone you can think of for information. This includes the U.S. Small Business Administration, the Internal Revenue Service, state and local government entities, trade organizations, small business organizations, and any other resource. You can ask for a list of their publications, services, and products relevant to your small business idea (and for start-ups in general). See chapter 13 for a variety of useful resources.

Gather this information and begin poring over it in anticipation of writing your business plan. Some of the information might also influence the final shape of your service or product.

Your research is also conducted in accordance with the questions we asked you in the first chapter. These can be used as a basis for general research on all aspects of business. In addition, ask your own unique questions and provide your own resources for answering them. Chapter 3 explains a variety of research resources and unique ideas. The results of steps 1 and 2 will culminate in a business plan.

Time Frame: It may take up to a month to order and receive SBA, IRS, and other publications and information, so do it early in the process. While waiting, you can meet with local resources such as SCORE officers or local businesses and suppliers. SCORE is a 501(c)(3) nonprofit organization that provides free business mentoring services to aspiring entrepreneurs.

Step 3: Make the Internet Work for You

From ordering a stack of business cards to marketing and advertising your business, the list of things that can be accomplished on the Internet grows with each passing month, and typically at a lower cost than most previous solutions.

The bottom line is that today you use the Internet to buy, and if you're a business owner, you certainly use it to sell.

It's critical to think about your company's online presence in the infancy of your planning process. While many experts think that traditional websites eventually won't be necessary thanks to the growth of such social media alternatives as Facebook, LinkedIn, and Twitter, it's a good idea to consider, at least for now, a conventional website that fits the attributes of your business and your need to reach the outside world.

You'll hear the word *content* a lot. Content is not just about a bunch of words on a website homepage. Today, web presence is not so much about the billboard approach but is more like a TV station approach. Dead air is unacceptable. A website might give you a kickoff point, but the key thing today is to get people talking about you online. Smart business owners make time to share critical messages, sales information, and even casual greetings a few times a week, not so much bombarding the customer as checking in.

But a good online presence involves some finesse and a real understanding of what you're trying to sell the customer. It's not a bad idea to consult with a public relations or web professional as you figure this out. A static web page may be one avenue, and daily posts on Facebook and Twitter (or whatever the next Facebook or Twitter are) may be another.

This is not a book about marketing or social media strategy, so we'll leave you with just one tip. Head to chapter 9, "Getting Social." We have a few basic research resources there that will get you rolling.

Step 4: Develop a Business Plan

The development of a business plan is a very important step and one you must do regardless of the size of your business. The creation of a business plan should be done after steps 1 and 2, but it really can be done concurrently or as you gather the information from your research. It might also overlap into some of the steps that follow.

The importance and scope of your plan depends on several factors, but all businesses should develop one. A detailed business plan outlines your business start-up and the first six months to one year of operation. It also includes projections for three, five, or ten years down the road, depending on your short- and long-term plans for the business and your personal life. This plan is your blueprint to guide your critical business decisions for the foreseeable future. You will want to be careful and thorough in its preparation.

QUICK Tip

Business Plans Vary: The size, type, and nature of your business will determine the depth and scope of your plan. The SBA, and in particular its SCORE program, may be able to lend technical and practical advice. Contact the SCORE office in your area (check chapter 14 for state-by-state listings) for more information. In addition, private companies provide consulting services to businesses in areas such as marketing, personnel, finance, and so on. Depending on your business, the cost of a personal consultant might be worth it.

The process of writing a business plan is discussed in more detail in chapter 4. Each part of a business plan defines and molds your business concept in one way or another. By thoroughly preparing each section, you will obtain that blueprint, which will also serve as a springboard to obtaining financing. With initiative, hard work, and patience, you will produce a great written business plan to guide your small business each step of the way.

 **Time Frame:** The time needed to develop a business plan depends on the factors mentioned already. For a SOHO business, you might need to spend two weeks to one month on your plan. For larger businesses, a month to several months may be needed, and it might be wise to seek outside help. Some people even spend a year writing and rewriting their plans until they are as thorough and professional as possible.

Figure 2.2: QUESTIONS FOR LEGAL, ACCOUNTING, AND FINANCIAL PLANNING PROFESSIONALS

If you need to consult a lawyer, an accountant, or a financial planner, keep in mind the following specific questions. These are by no means exhaustive, but they will at least get you started in the right direction.

Ask All Three:

❑ Do you have general thoughts on my business idea?

❑ Is my choice of organization type right, in your opinion?

Ask an Attorney:

❑ What forms need to be filed for certain entity types? Make a list of them and ask him or her to explain the purpose of each.

❑ What zoning or commerce regulations are there in my chosen field of business?

❑ Are there any other local restrictions?

❑ What services can you offer after I start my business? What are your fees?

Ask an Accountant:

❑ What is the tax effect of choosing various entity types?

❑ What taxes do various entity types need to plan for?

❑ When do I need to pay them?

❑ How do I pay them?

Continued

❑ **How should I handle accounting?**

❑ **When should my accounting year begin and end?**

Ask a Financial Planner:

❑ **Considering my current income, spending, and debt, am I ready to start an independent business?**

❑ **Should my spouse be doing anything different with his or her finances or career as I prepare to start a business?**

❑ **Given the kind of business I'm preparing to open, how much money should I have in reserve to take care of personal and family expenses?**

❑ **What kind of insurance or other protections should I have in place to make sure my family is protected in case I die or the business goes bust?**

❑ **How do I safeguard my savings, particularly for my kids' college funds?**

Step 5: Consult a Lawyer, an Accountant, and a Financial Planner

You may need a lawyer and an accountant for consultation on legal and tax issues that are directly connected to the business. A financial planner can help you coordinate the money issues that bridge your personal and business life, and you will be surprised how often these issues arise.

Attorneys and accountants can be of great help in many areas, especially when it comes to dealing with government regulations and small business legal issues. The SOHO may not need any consultations except when issues of zoning or regulations come up. If you intend to form any other entity, you might want to see an accountant for tax consultations and a lawyer for specific legal advice on regulations, state requirements, and licensing information.

Try visiting business lawyers and accountants who handle small businesses. They may have more detailed information for you. In addition,

QUICK Tip

Finding a Financial Planner: The Financial Planning Association offers an online search feature for financial planners and their specialties in all fifty states. It's wise to interview several planners and to ask about their experience working with clients who also operate small businesses. Go to http://www.fpanet.org to use the PlannerSearch feature.

if you cannot afford either, some communities have a low-cost incubator and/or quasi-governmental business consulting centers that offer assistance.

A financial planner is a trained professional who advises on personal financial issues, and we feel that a consultation regarding your personal finances is crucial before starting any business. It is always advisable to make sure that your savings, investments, and assets are protected before you take the substantial risk of starting a company. If you have a lot of debt, you may want to wait until it's paid off before taking on the risk of a company.

Parallel financial planning should be done for personal as well as business finances, and everyone's situation is unique. That's why it's wise to contact a financial planner who can examine your preparations from both perspectives.

Take your business plan to the lawyer, accountant, and financial planner so that each can review it. This will give them a better understanding of your business and your goals.

These three sets of experts can also weigh in on your choice of business entity, which is essentially the legal structure for your business. Each

Time Frame: After you have completed an initial draft of your business plan, you should talk to a professional accountant and lawyer to get their perspectives on what you've done. When making the appointment with either the accountant or the attorney, ask about fees and services, and particularly what one to three hours of initial consulting time will cost. You may or may not want to hire this person to help you with the legal and/or financial side of your start-up going forward.

business entity has its own operating, licensing, and tax considerations and therefore must be weighed against your personal finances first so you can pick the right entity for your business financial structure.

Step 6: Determine Your Business Entity

After you confer with your team of experts, you'll decide which legal entity is best for your business. Although some states differ with regard to organizational names and features, most offer the following basic business registrations:

- Sole proprietor
- General partnership
- Limited liability partnership (LLP)
- Limited liability companies (LLC)
- Corporations, either C (regular) or S (subchapter S), profit or non-profit, close corporation or professional corporations

Determining your business entity depends on many factors, including tax liability and rates (again, this affects your personal finances as well as your business finances), legal liability needs, business size, business type, capital (lack or possession of), personal preferences, needs, and/or future business plans.

When you sit down to determine your business, think about what you will be doing and which types of business entities best protect your interests with the minimum of government interference and taxation.

QUICK Tip

Finding the Right Person for the Job: How do you find the right attorney, accountant, or financial planner? Personal referrals are best—if you know someone already in business who has had good experience with advisers, ask for their contact information. Failing that, go to chapter 14, turn to your state of residency, and check the listing under your state bar or certified public accountant association's online search service for attorneys or certified public accountants (check the earlier tip to find a financial planner). These online listings allow you to plug in your specific needs and find professionals who best fit the profile you're looking for. Make sure you interview them before you hire them.

Time Frame: Depending on the complexity of your business, your research on your company's legal entity may take anywhere from a couple of days to a few weeks. Make sure you consult the right professionals before making your final decision.

Sole proprietorships and partnerships are fairly uncomplicated business structures, whereas limited liability companies and corporations have more requirements and legal obligations. Each type is examined in chapter 5, where a list of pluses and minuses rates each entity type. Your lawyer and accountant can help you make this decision if you're still unsure.

Small office and home office businesses are often the simplest business to categorize because their needs are the simplest. If you start an at-home business, be aware that you may need liability protection or the structure offered by a more complex business entity (and you may need insurance on top of that). Although there are requirement and cost differences between simple and complex entities, you should not sacrifice your business needs for the sake of simplicity or cost.

Step 7: Seek Government Help

After researching and writing your business plan, consulting professionals, and solidifying your business entity, you might want to pursue this optional step. Consultation with your local SBA or SCORE office might provide you with further sources of government assistance. A SOHO business might pursue this step in lieu of seeing accountants or lawyers, if only to save money. In addition, these government organizations can advise you on how to obtain loans, start-up assistance, local information, minority and women's business assistance, and practical advice (especially from SCORE officers). Chapter 13 lists the various U.S. Small Business Administration programs and services. Appendix A lists SBA publications.

These agencies deal with small and new businesses every day and can provide you with expert and friendly advice. At SCORE, retired business executives will try to assist you and answer questions or concerns you might have.

Time Frame: Seek governmental help or consultation around the same time you see your lawyer, accountant, and/or financial planner. It might help if you know what entity you will become before seeing them; however, they may also be able to help you make that decision.

Step 8: Start Your Business

Now that you know what type of business entity you are set to become, the next thing to do is file the necessary forms and pay any filing and/or licensing fees. Chapter 14's state-by-state guide will give you referral information to find out which essential and optional filings may be necessary for the particular entity and type of business you plan to run.

If you need a lawyer to assist you, he or she will start preparing the necessary forms on the basis of the information you share during your first visit. If you are incorporating, you may or may not have certain information available, including company name, directors, and other features. If some of that information is still to be determined, you may need to schedule a second visit or a phone conference (make sure you understand the fees for both options). The forms will be available for you to sign within a few weeks and may be mailed to you.

Read all forms carefully, and do not be afraid to ask the attorney questions. Always make sure either you or your lawyer fills out any necessary state forms such as sales tax ID number forms (if those are required for your business) or any withholding forms and licensing paperwork. In some cases, it may be recommended that you apply for an Employer Identification Number (EIN) by filing Form SS-4 to aid in tax reporting.

Again, depending on your business entity and your state requirements, your state revenue department will likely register you for withholding, sales and use tax, and other necessary taxes.

Local requirements range from city or county business licenses and permits to city or county tax registration—this is information you'll need to check on your own in the city where you live. Your local officials will help you through the process. Usually, you will contact the county clerk, recorder, city clerk, or revenue office, depending on your city or state. Your local Yellow Pages will provide the proper local numbers to call.

The final stage of this step is to get a business checking account at a local bank or credit union. Shop around for value and service. The fees and services vary from bank to bank and between large and small banks. Use a reputable bank that you feel comfortable with. Your bank will be important to you, so it is important to build a positive relationship with it.

Time Frame: The legal and accounting launch phase for your business may take up to one month for the whole process to be finished. You can speed it along by using expedited services, which many states offer for an additional fee. You must start a separate bank account to handle business-related finances once you begin the start-up process.

Step 9: Seek Sources of Financing—If You Really Need It

Seeking financing is the final step, because no one except your mother will invest in your business if it is not a legal entity. Once you have established your small business, you can begin the process of obtaining funding. Several potential financial resources are fully discussed in chapter 8. Banks, the SBA, private foundations, angel investors, venture capitalists, stockholders, business associates, other businesses, and friends and family are all possible sources of financing.

As for the reality of getting loans from banks or private investors, at the time of publication for this edition, the financing environment was still very tough. The global financial collapse in 2008 redefined what had previously been a relatively loose lending process for entrepreneurs.

Since this step is done after starting your business entity, you will have your business plan and business structure established. You will want to look, act, and be professional in every aspect of this endeavor. This will allow potential investors a look at your plans. Start-up funding is very hard to get, however, so you may have to use sources close to you—yourself, friends, family—until your business grows enough to be attractive to a bank or private investor. Selling stock by direct public offering (DPO; the first offering is often referred to as an initial public offering, or IPO) is one way a new small business can get funding, and it is growing in popularity.

QUICK Tip

Personal and Business Finances: For many small business people, particularly sole proprietors, personal and business finances tend to be intertwined. So if you want to qualify for loan or investment assistance at start-up or down the road, clean up your credit report and make sure your personal finances are in good shape as the first step to starting your business.

Most states have specific laws and requirements to follow if you do a DPO, and you should consult an attorney before doing so.

In your search for funding, don't forget to stay motivated even when you are rejected (and you will be). The bank that turns you down today may give you a loan after you have proved that you can run your business successfully.

Technically, there is one more step: start operating your business! Get things rolling as soon as you can. The old adage that time is money is true—especially for a small business.

Time Frame: The time period for seeking sources of financing varies, as you may or may not get a loan or start-up capital. This depends on you, your plan, and whom you see for capital. To speed things along, gather all of your tax and financial documents for the past three years so you don't have to chase these bits of information around while the bank is waiting.

Figure 2.3: THE NINE GREAT STEPS CHECKLIST

Write down the date that you complete each step.

❏ Step 1: Determine Your Product or Service
   Date Completed: _____

❏ Step 2: Research Your Idea
   Date Completed: _____

❏ Step 3: Make the Internet Work for You
   Date Completed: _____

❏ Step 4: Develop a Business Plan
   Date Completed: _____

❏ Step 5: Consult a Lawyer, an Accountant, and a Financial Planner
   Date Completed: _____

❏ Step 6: Determine Your Business Entity
   Date Completed: _____

❏ Step 7: Seek Government Help
   Date Completed: _____

❏ Step 8: Start Your Business (File All Necessary Forms)
 • Federal Identification Number Registration
   Date Completed: _____
 • State/Local Business Registration
   Date Completed: _____
 • State Tax Registration
   Date Completed: _____

❏ Step 9: Seek Sources of Financing
   Date Completed: _____

Notes:_____

_____

_____

_____

_____

_____

_____

_____

_____

_____

Chapter 3

Defining the Business

▶ **Researching and documenting your start-up needs**

▶ **How to gather information**

▶ **Considering the transition to self-employment**

This chapter will help you begin the process of defining your business and the amount of time, capital, and organization you will need to launch it. You'll be getting further into the creation of your business plan, as well as discovering answers to even more important questions.

Researching and Documenting Your Start-Up Needs

Researching everything about your chosen business, from regulations to start-up requirements to sources of capital to suppliers, is vital. Much of your research will be predicated on one simple question: what don't I know?

In chapter 1, you answered a battery of questions. Hopefully, you came up with many more of your own. At this stage, you'll be conducting more extensive research to find those answers, statistics, and information.

If you are unsure about which type of business you want to be in, research several, compile a complete list of all the good and bad points of each, and decide which is likely to be more successful. After your specific idea is developed, we recommend taking six steps to thoroughly research your business proposition, as shown in figure 3.1.

QUICK Tip

Research: When it comes to research, don't leave any stones unturned. Smart entrepreneurs spend weeks researching their business—at the library, at the bookstore, on the Internet, and at government agencies (particularly SCORE or your closest Small Business Development Center office; see chapter 14). Don't forget to check with your local Chamber of Commerce or industry-specific associations and groups—networking will be a necessity no matter what business you choose to operate. Most of all, study competing businesses to get an idea of what works and doesn't.

Figure 3.1: **THE SIX STEPS OF START-UP RESEARCH**

1. List your personal goals first.

Building on what you did in chapter 1, conscientiously write down what you want to do with your life. List your likes, dislikes, and goals (for your financial life and your family life). Take a great deal of time with this and be thorough. The more honest you are with yourself, the more realistic you will be about your business goals. Be sure to list where you want to be in three, five, and ten years. Start a separate assessment of your personal finances—debt, savings, investments, health and personal insurance, and so on—before you start any business, to make sure that your home life is protected no matter what happens with the business.

2. List your business goals.

Write down your short- and long-term goals for your business. Ask yourself the questions from chapter 1 to help shape and mold those goals. Be sure to include any questions you have developed on your own. You may not have answers to all of the questions or you may be dissatisfied with some of the answers, and that will spur you to further research. Don't forget about an "exit plan"—the dates and circumstances under which you would exit the business by choice or by necessity.

3. Compare your goals.

Consider the compatibility of the goals in the first item with those in the second item, and determine which businesses will most be able to satisfy your personal and professional goals. Often, your personal goals will dictate your professional goals.

4. Research extensively.

Remember that researching a start-up has much to do with the customer base, industry, and the competitive cycle in which you plan to operate your business. If your customer base is primarily local, you'll be looking to research your business concept against local competitors and business cycles. If your customer base is statewide, national, or potentially global, then you have to research for that level of reach

Continued

as well. To help you, resources are scattered throughout this book, and particularly in chapters 13 and 14, but don't ignore resources like business reference sections in public and university libraries that you can use for free. The Internet won't provide everything.

5. Analyze the data and information.

After you have gathered your important information in one place, take some time alone or with your business partner(s) to pore over it. Your research should provide answers to soothe your nervousness or apprehensions, and it will provide the framework for your all-important business plan, covered in the next chapter.

6. Re-research.

After you have gathered your information, you may discover that you need still more facts or answers. Why? Because your research will inevitably raise new questions that need new answers. Don't be alarmed—this is normal. Any process as involved as starting a business is bound to be complex and time consuming, and you must be flexible enough to work with that complexity. If that means burning the midnight oil to pursue more answers, do it. In the end, you'll be happy you did.

How to Gather Information

Now that you have spent time with figure 3.1, you probably see that researching can be accomplished in many different ways and with many different resources.

Luckily, we live in the information age, where the click of a mouse can bring a wealth of information to your computer screen. Information is at your fingertips just waiting to be discovered. The resources and methods listed here are diverse and, in some cases, unique. This should give you an edge on your small business start-up competitors. Many more specific resources are listed in chapter 13:

• Visit your local library, bookstore, or newsstand, all of which contain further resources that will greatly aid your search. Libraries have business sections and most catalog systems are computerized, which makes interlibrary searching and loaning easier. Bookstores can be an even bigger help with current titles (check the business best-seller list on Amazon.com and the *New York Times* to see whether any titles fit your search). Print and online resources are listed in chapter 13.

- Use the Small Business Administration's many agencies and programs. Along with the SBA, other government entities provide business information. In addition, the vast online library on the SBA's website contains a section with small business success stories.

- Talk to a retired executive at the Service Corps of Retired Executives (SCORE), an organization funded by the SBA. These men and women can be very helpful in using their experience and knowledge to aid your research.

- Depending on your business, use demographic data such as traffic counts, population statistics, crime data, census figures, tax rates, buying trends, and so on, to get a sense of how your customer base behaves and, most important, where they are.

- Conduct market studies and surveys. You can do this yourself, either formally or informally, to get feedback on your product or service. If you have the money, you can hire a firm to do this for you.

- Spy. That's right—if you want to know about prices at another store or how many customers a competitor has, simply visit the store and walk around, observing it in action. This is a model that can also be adapted in businesses other than retail. Just make sure you're able to do this legally.

- If you have the opportunity to get a job in the particular kind of business you would like to start someday—even a part-time job—consider it. You'll get a feel for the work everyone associated with the company does, and most important, you'll see what the owner deals with every day and whether you can successfully deal with those challenges.

- Attend trade shows, expos, and business fairs specific to your industry. These are excellent sources of information and personal contacts, and they allow you to scan what competition is out there.

- Network with colleagues, friends, and associates. Everyone knows someone else who can help with some aspect of their business. Use these friends and associates and their knowledge to your best advantage. Most will be glad to share advice with you.

- Visit local colleges to see whether they have any resources that might help you start a small business. Many campuses are sites of the SBA program's Small Business Development Centers. Colleges may also offer some demographic and economic data.

- Evaluate competitor and potential employee profiles on LinkedIn to get a sense of experience and background in the industry of your choice.
- Follow the local and national news. Keep abreast of trends and fads. Often, your local papers contain a wealth of small business news in your community.
- Talk to members of your local chamber of commerce. Again, they will probably be open to helping you along. They were once in your situation, and they might be happy to share any knowledge they have picked up along the way.
- Use the Internet to open the door to a wide selection of small business and helpful government websites. The beauty of the Internet is that one site often leads to another, which leads you to sources that you may never have thought of on your own.
- Talk to other entrepreneurs who have started their own businesses for advice, information, and encouragement. Many small business owners will gladly tell you what they went through.
- If you are creating a physical product, examine your competitors' goods, marketing, and advertising programs.
- Talk to your competition's former employees. They may give you insight into how the competition operates.
- Brainstorm with a knowledgeable colleague, friend, or spouse to vet your concept and to come up with other questions that you must answer before getting your business off the ground.
- Attend continuing education courses, often taught by local universities. These refresher courses may contain information or contacts that make them well worth your time.
- Attend meetings for and eventually consider joining professional organizations and associations in your chosen industry. Not only will you get the chance to network and get your product known, but also you'll likely meet talented management and potential employees.
- Read trade publications. Most industries have specific print and online publications that give more in-depth coverage of your chosen industry than general news and broadcast outlets.
- Get to know bankers, accountants, and attorneys as you plan your company. They can discuss lending, tax, and legal issues informally until you are ready to discuss your business at a later stage.
- Visit your local government's economic development department for information on finances and available programs.

- Listen to talk-radio business programs and watch business shows on television, but keep in mind that you should verify all information you hear.
- Join barter exchanges to exchange goods and services via barter if it will make sense for your business. Bartering saves money and can be a good networking tool—and it is akin to networking.
- Consider hiring a business consultant in your field. This is expensive, but if you have the money, a consultant might be able to help you start your business on a great footing.
- If you are a woman or a minority, work with organizations that help these groups.
- Check appendix A for information on great start-up publications from the SBA.
- Last but not least, if you don't read much now, realize that reading will become a regular activity when you run a business. Learn as much as you can about your local, national, and global economy, because these trends will affect your business no matter how small you are.

If you can satisfactorily answer the motivational questions confronting you and you have done your research, then you will be intellectually ready to be the head of your own business. But there is one more step.

Considering the Transition to Self-Employment

Going into business is more than a financial and career commitment. It's also a personal commitment and one that begs an answer to the most visceral of questions in the business development process: am I really going to love this major change I'm about to make in my life?

Because it really does have to be about love. It's that kind of commitment.

Some new business owners end their old career on a Friday and start their companies on Monday. That's fine. But we think it's a good idea to make business ownership a real transition over weeks, months, or years so that you are adequately capitalized; so that your personal finances are in order; and, most important, so that you have enough research and real-time experience invested in your concept that you know for certain this new business will build traction over time and be work that you will enjoy.

So what's to consider? Plenty:

- **Parallel planning of personal and business finances:** We're not talking about commingling personal and business finances—you will need to set up separate record keeping for both. But this is a more basic question. Many businesses take weeks, months, or years to become profitable. Can your personal finances sustain a period of time when you might not be getting a salary or when you might be shoring up the business with money you've set aside for that purpose? Is your spouse or partner ready to support the household while you support the business? Will you be able to pay the mortgage? What about other debts? Will you be able to continue saving for your retirement first and your children's college education second? You will hear us say this many times throughout this book, but the time to organize and stress test your personal finances is before you start a company, not afterward.

QUICK Tip

What's a Financial Stress Test? You'll hear the term *financial stress test* plenty in business finance, but it's worth applying to your personal finances. It helps to coordinate this activity with an accountant or qualified financial planner, but essentially the process is all about developing a list of worst-case scenarios about starting up a company ("What if the business fails?" is a question that should be on everyone's list) and determining whether your personal finances will withstand the risk you'll introduce in your life by starting up a company. It's also important to eliminate personal debt and maximize savings before you go into business.

- **Working part-time for yourself first:** Many small businesses get their start as part-time enterprises for which founders work nights and weekends to get the company off the ground and/or set up shifts with friends, family, or employees to staff more hours in the day as the business gets established. Again, it depends on the type of business you're considering, but keeping your day job while starting a new business can be a good idea, because it will secure an income stream while you're getting the business on its feet.
- **Setting up the end game now:** Too many people look at a business as a job, not as a bridge to their future. What do we mean by this?

If you're working for an employer now, do you consider yourself in control of that business? Of course not. The owner's in control. Well, when you start a business, you become the man or woman in charge. So it's time to start thinking that way. You will control the destiny of that enterprise on behalf of yourself, your family, your employees, and your customers. So you need to do long-term planning that will benefit all those constituencies instead of thinking about whether you'll make enough money to stay open this month. Before you open your doors, start by thinking ten, twenty, or thirty years ahead. What kind of life do you want the day you sell, close, or pass down that business? Setting these goals now will give you an even broader picture of what you want your business to accomplish over time and the life you want to have at its end. That's what we mean by setting an end game before you start the company—no one can do it but you. And there's an added bonus—having an end game will definitely help you focus your business plan.

Although it's never been easy, millions of people before you have started their own businesses. Not all succeeded, but not all failed. When armed with research, months of preplanning, a killer business plan, and dedication, the entrepreneur enters the world of business with a decided advantage. It is this advantage early on that may be the difference between success and frustration, which can lead directly to failure. You will put this advantage to good use in the next chapter.

Chapter

4

Your First Business Plan

▶ **Gathering the elements for a successful small business plan**

▶ **Writing the business plan**

▶ **The key sections of a business plan**

Any successful business launch, particularly one that requires reaching out to lenders or investors, requires a solid business plan. As the business evolves, there will be short- and long-term strategic plans that build on that initial vision.

These strategic plans are different from your initial business plan, although the two are related. In college, the keystone class in the business program is often a strategic planning course, and for good reason. Planning is the key to small business success.

There are two essential reasons to write a business plan. First, writing out a business plan helps establish the shape and potential of a business in your mind. Second, you will have a document to get lenders and investors interested in your business so it has the proper amount of capital to grow over time.

Many people who operate home-based businesses with either little or no need for financing might wonder whether they need to write a business plan. The answer? It's always a good idea because it will force you to consider all the features and needs of your business, and maybe some new ideas and efficiencies along the way.

In short, it's a way to examine your business idea thoroughly before you take on the risk, and that's never a bad idea. It is necessary to plan, chart, and dream about the future of your potential business. Without a vision, a business is blindfolded and will go around in circles until it finally collapses. History is littered with blindfolded entities— businesses, people, and even countries—that had no direction, plan, or long-term goals.

Your first business plan will be your blueprint for operations, financing, and growth. It will provide a guide to running and managing your company, as well as to marketing your goods or services. The plan is an integral part of your quest for financing and capital, as it forecasts needed start-up and operating capital. As you project into the future, your anticipated growth patterns will be laid out, which makes goal setting easier to achieve.

Gathering the Elements for a Successful Small Business Plan

Before you write your plan, consider how important it will be to your start-up. Although the size of a plan may vary from a few pages to a few

Get the Order Right: Experts always tell you to write the introduction, executive summary, and conclusion of your business plan after you've completed all other sections. Saving these sections until you are done will give you the perspective you need to write them well.

hundred, you need not worry about how big it is, just how thorough it is for your needs. We believe in writing and rewriting, so leave time to create and refine this plan, and consider key dates and deadlines in the progression of your future business or service.

You're writing for a specific readership—potential financial backers who need to be impressed by your professionalism and thoroughness. Because the plan is the blueprint for your business, you must blend accuracy and realism with the ability to tell a compelling story about your idea.

Don't write your business plan in a vacuum. Spend the time you need to brainstorm with trusted and knowledgeable colleagues and financial experts as you research your plan. As you're writing drafts, make sure that those colleagues see your revisions. See chapter 13 for a list of a few books that offer extensive advice on business plans, with sample plans for you to browse.

We'll get to the structure of the plan in a minute, but there are some critical things you need to know before you even sit down to write.

Come Up with an Idea

The business idea is the center of the whole effort. What are you trying to do? How does your idea exceed what the competition is doing? What's the better mousetrap you're trying to build?

The more original the idea, the more passionate you will be about it, and the harder you'll work at it. Microsoft founder Bill Gates and Google founders Sergey Brin and Larry Page love what they do and are good at it. That's not an accident—it is motivation and drive based on a passion for their businesses.

The simplest of entities (a small retail store, for example) could mean the world to you, and that will make you work very hard to make it a success. You do not need to run a multimillion-dollar company to be a happy business owner. Being creative and developing a unique product can often bring about great success.

Time Frame: Coming up with a solid business idea could take years, but to create a simple corporation, it usually takes three to six weeks to file and return all necessary state registrations and forms. It's wise not to actually conduct business until all necessary approvals are officially documented.

QUICK Tip

Keep Learning: Banks, your local Small Business Development Center (check your state's listing in chapter 14), universities, and consulting firms often offer free- and low-cost workshops, classes, and podcasts on the process of creating a business plan. In-person courses can also be a great networking opportunity.

Choose a Name

You will also need to name your company. Remember, many states maintain that the words *Corporation, Incorporated, Inc., Company,* or *Co.* must appear in the title of the corporation name at the time of registration or possibly all signage and collateral. Limited partnerships usually must have *LP* or *Limited Partnership* in the name. Any required words must be included in the name the company uses for business purposes. That is to say, if a person or company writes you a check, make sure it is made out to the full name of the company so that it agrees with your bank records.

In addition, many states require that the name of the company be somehow identifiable with the owners. Assumed or fictitious names are sometimes used for companies, proprietors, or partnerships not wishing to identify the owners in the name of the company that customers deal with. Some businesses are allowed to "do business as" (DBA) under a different name from their company name. Go to chapter 14 to contact the state agency that handles these matters.

Define Your Purpose and Goals

A vital step is to conscientiously map out your mission and first-year goals. Your purpose should be clear and concise, yet it may not have to be so clear on the certificate of incorporation. And remember to ask those very important questions from chapter 1, including the following:

1. How much capital will we need?
2. How much do we have?

The answers to these questions will directly affect your company's operations, so make sure that you know what they are before you present your plan to potential funders or investors.

List Your Officers and Their Duties

Corporations typically have to register the names of a board of directors. Boards are a group of people who have oversight authority over top management. You'll hear that duty referred to as governance responsibility. Boards become increasingly important depending on the size of the company and the involvement of outside investors and lenders.

QUICK Tip

Boards of Directors: Still confused about boards? This is why new business owners are wise to consult with a tax expert and an attorney before launching their company. The kind, size, industry, and location of your business are factors in how you form and run the company and the amount of board oversight that will be involved. That's why customized advice matters.

Find an Office and Agent

You will need an office and an agent, often called a resident agent if you go the corporate or LLC route. The agent is the business or person who can receive legal papers on behalf of a corporation. Typically, the agent who incorporates for you is a lawyer, but not necessarily, and his or her address must be on the document. The address of the company is usually an office, although it can be a home if you are zoned business or commercial or are permitted to operate a business at your residence under local or state law.

QUICK Tip

Finance: Not a finance whiz? Start learning. While experts—lawyers, accountants, and financial planners—are valuable parts of an entrepreneur's team, you can't leave all the numbers work to them. Take a basic finance course at a community college, and keep making time to learn as you go along in business. This will keep you realistic while budgeting and help you avoid costly mistakes later on.

Plan Your Capital Requirements

You need to realize that undercapitalization is a major problem for small businesses, and it's critical to plan cash and reserve needs before you create a business. Sources of capital are listed in chapter 8.

If you need $25,000 for your business, don't settle for $2,500 and try to make do. It simply will not work. Try to raise as much as you can, and see whether you can use that cushion as leverage to borrow the rest. By cutting short your capital infusion into your company, you may also cut short its life.

QUICK Tip

The Business Environment: The latest edition of this book was being edited during the slow recovery period from the 2008 crash. While big business lending was recovering, small businesses and start-ups were having a difficult time borrowing at all. This is part of your due diligence in any business start-up process. Read, watch, and—most importantly—talk to people who may be in a position to invest or finance your business and determine how realistic that environment may be for you.

Determine Your Start-Up Equipment Needs

Whatever your equipment needs are for your new business, definitely shop around for what you need, and consider buying used if you can. Online resources can help you compare prices on a host of products, and don't ignore live and online auctions for great pricing on new or used items. As cold as it sounds, someone else's failure might be a ticket to your success.

And remember, you don't need to have the flashiest office space or furniture when you're starting out. Most cities auction off old municipal equipment from time to time, and these auctions are a great place to pick up everything from desks to computers to filing cabinets. Law enforcement departments at the local, state, and federal levels also auction everything from business machinery to vehicles. See chapter 13 for information on other sources of equipment and supplies.

Location, Location, Location

Again, as this book was being revised, the commercial and residential real estate markets were in real trouble. Bad for sellers, but great for buyers and renters looking for bargains and alternative space to operate a business.

In any market, it pays to get to know brokers and real estate investors who are familiar with the full range of commercial space in your community, if in fact you do need commercial space (the SOHO movement is definitely convincing many entrepreneurs otherwise). Local business journals tend to measure the commercial real estate market on the ground level, so it's easier to get an idea of pricing.

Also, see whether local governments are stepping in to help commercial landlords fill empty space. Government subsidies and declaration of enterprise zones tend to lower rent against most commercial alternatives, at least for a while. One possible way to obtain cheaper office space (and some government assistance) is to locate in an urban enterprise zone. Although the terms may differ from city to city, the purpose does not. These zones are often located in older, inner-city areas, and their intention is to pump money back into the blighted area in hopes of improvement. Often, the government will give tax breaks, grants, or other assistance to companies that locate and hire in these areas. It is certainly something to look into. Call your city's mayoral office or economic development office to find out more.

In addition, some cities have "incubators," or business development centers. These are usually full-service centers that offer your new business receptionists, office space, conference rooms, equipment, and so on, without the usual high costs. They are intended to aid new businesses in the initial stages of incorporation. The incubator can be of valuable assistance, especially if you have limited start-up and operating funds. Incubators are often run by local or state governments, and many are run in conjunction with the SBA, which has a large number of Small Business Development Centers. Check your city government directory or the SBA's website, or call your local chamber of commerce for information.

Writing the Business Plan

You've got the details. Now it's time to start writing.

The writing process will uncover many more questions about your idea, and you'll likely need to do more research as you write. Yes, it sounds like a process that will never be finished, and in a way that's true—you never stop researching and planning in business, or at least you shouldn't.

But the process of actually writing a draft of the plan, whether you're an experienced writer or you've never attempted to write one before, is extremely beneficial because it helps you focus on what you really want to do with your business.

Focus on the short term in your plan, but plan for the long term. Your plan is a blueprint for your first few years of operation, but it also forecasts future growth. This is done to preserve your sense of both short- and long-term planning and to present potential investors with two things: your short-term operating goals and your long-term vision.

The plan should not be unrealistic, though. Leave your dreams out of it, but by all means include your goals. Just make sure that they are obtainable and down to earth. Bankers, venture capitalists, and investors know impossible dreams when they see them, and they will pass you over if your goals are in the clouds.

A business plan has several parts to it. We listed them in figure 4.1 below and include brief explanations on the purpose and importance of each section. For further in-depth analysis of a plan, check out one of the resources in chapter 13, and don't forget to use appendixes B and C in your thought and outline process.

Now that you've studied figure 4.1, you are ready to think about what goes into each part of the plan. Remember, your plan will vary depending on your size, goals, and entity type. The key words here are *thoroughness* and *realism*, and when it comes to projections, *precision*.

Just keep in mind that there is no set time to write a business plan. It will depend on factors ranging from the type and needs of the business you're trying to open to the actual time you have to research and write

---

Figure 4.1: **BUSINESS PLAN ESSENTIALS**

Business plans are very adaptable to a specific business's situation, but all contain some common elements. Your business plan should include the following sections:

- ❏ **Cover sheet**
- ❏ **Executive summary**
- ❏ **Mission statement**
- ❏ **Business concept**
- ❏ **The management team**
- ❏ **Industry analysis**
- ❏ **Financial analysis, goals, and objectives**
- ❏ **Day-to-day operations**
- ❏ **Financing needs**
- ❏ **Summary**
- ❏ **Appendix**

---

it. It's not a Ph.D. dissertation—which means it shouldn't take years to write—but by the time you're done, you should know the answers to virtually every question that you or your investors will potentially have about your business.

The Key Sections of a Business Plan

We'll say this over and over. Write for your audience. What follows is a general structure for writing a business plan, but do whatever you can to investigate what successful business plans look like for the industry and audience you're writing for. No question is silly if it means the difference between getting the money and support to launch the business and not getting a dime.

Where to get this information? Network with peers in your industry.

It's Not All Smooth Sailing: a business plan should be optimistic but never shy away from addressing the risks involved in your business idea. Be upfront and honest, and do not avoid the problem areas. If you are looking for lenders or investors, they won't be shy about picking apart your work.

Talk to local business professors. Talk to your personal experts—certified public accountants and attorneys. And if you meet potential funders, ask them what they want to see in a business plan. Better yet, ask them what they hate to see in a business plan—you'll hopefully get an emotional response that will teach you a lot.

Cover Sheet
The cover sheet simply contains the name of your company; the address; and contact information for key managers (you and anyone else running the firm) including phone, email, and U.S. mailing address.

Executive Summary
This is both an introduction and an encapsulation of the plan, but you should write it at the end, after you've had the chance to create the rest of the document. An executive summary should be no longer than one page, and it should summarize the business, its products and services, risks, opportunities, target strategies, competition, financing needs, and—finally—your projected return on investment.

Mission Statement
The mission statement of your plan is a one- or two-sentence statement that describes the purpose and culture of your business and its goals. It is as much for you as for potential lenders and investors, because it encapsulates your overall company philosophy and direction. It should communicate the kind of business you will run and how the public will perceive you.

QUICK Tip

Brief Is Beautiful: As you've probably guessed, everyone's attention span is shorter now than ever before. That includes professionals whose work it is to determine whether a business is worth an investment or a loan. This isn't a book to teach you how to write, but in the production of a business plan, it's hard to go wrong if your research is good, your facts are correct, and your wording is clear and concise. Writing an effective business plan really isn't much different from any kind of successful writing. You need to carefully determine what you need to say, and then say it clearly and concisely so you don't waste your reader's time. Be prepared to do multiple drafts, and find trusted, experienced people to read it before you submit it formally to anyone. And even though this is your baby, accept criticisms and suggestions gracefully and with an open mind.

Another way to look at the mission statement is that it should read as if a loyal customer were describing your company. It should emphasize the uniqueness of your product, service, methods of doing business, commitment to quality and the customer, and overall integrity.

Mission statements vary depending on the type of business, but all contain information about the values of the company, a description of the goods or services, and a statement of customer service objectives. Often, they contain information on relevant technologies and/or practices that make the company unique—and better than the competition.

Business Concept

This business concept section will be written largely on the strength of your answers from chapter 1 and your follow-up research. This is the broad description of your business, broken down into specific parts as you see them. Again, thoroughness will apply. You will need to identify your start-up objectives and requirements, office location, personnel needs, and product and/or service identification and description. List your objectives at the one-year point (or longer, if that's common for your industry) and how you plan to get there. List your personnel requirements, which should be based on your examination of how many employees you will need and what their skill levels must be. You may need employees with skills you do not possess. A strength and weakness evaluation of your own skills will tell you what type of employees you need.

The Management Team

Who will run the business, and how qualified are they to do so? Depending on the size of the team, create an organizational chart that lists managers and defines their functions. Pay attention to which strengths are needed in each management position. A SOHO business may have only one employee, and that's fine. Just be sure to explain your reasoning, no matter how many employees you plan to have.

Other items include a description of the product or service you are offering, including how it is different from or better than what is already out there. If there is a board of directors, you must also identify its members. Include biographies of all relevant members of the team in the appendix, which will come at the end of your business plan and will also include any supporting documents or charts you may have to support your arguments.

QUICK Tip

Advisory Boards: It helps to have as many great minds as possible involved with a fledgling business. Many technology companies have discovered the concept of an advisory board—not a full-fledged board of directors with real governance responsibilities (that might come later), but a group of experienced individuals who provide counsel on a regular basis as the company is growing. Identify them, mention why their qualifications are of benefit to you, and include their biographies in the appendix.

Industry Analysis

The industry analysis section gives an informed overview of market share, leadership, players, market shifts, costs, pricing, and competition, which provide the opportunity for the new company's success.

Report on the health of the local, state, regional, and national economy as it relates generally and specifically to your business and industry. Discuss such things as seasonal economic fluctuations vis-à-vis your company and how the economy will affect you. A discussion of your industry and internal and external effects on it is warranted here.

List its growth trends, legal issues, strengths, and weaknesses. Your part in this industry may be affected by the whole industry's health.

Financial Analysis, Goals, and Objectives

The section on financial analysis, goals, and objectives is the portion of your business plan that bankers and potential investors will read most closely. Often, it's what outsiders will turn to first—they want to see the numbers. Expect to be grilled intensively on this section.

Remember that people who invest and lend generally tend to be experienced at zeroing in on problems and holes in a business plan. Be ready for them. Unless you have training in finance, it is wise to seek help from someone with experience in preparing this section.

This section of the business plan outlines the complete financial state of the business thus far. It indicates in detail your current financial state as an individual, and the current capital requirements and start-up costs for the business. It also outlines the short-term (one- to three-year) growth targets for the company.

QUICK Tip

Tailoring the Business Plan: Always be willing to tailor your business plan to a prospective audience the way you would a résumé for a prospective employer. If you are meeting with bankers, angels, or venture capital investors, don't be shy about asking about the structure of the plan they want to see. Yes, that might mean doing some rewrites for a specific audience or prospect. But that's what you do in business.

Again, you're writing a business plan that fits a particular industry and lender or investor audience. That will determine some elements of structure in this section. But generally, it's wise to start with a beginning balance sheet that gives readers a snapshot of your personal and/or business net worth on the date of the report. You will want to include a beginning balance sheet. List your assets (e.g., cash, receivables, prepaid expenses), liabilities (debts and accounts payable), and equity (stock values).

Then come projections. Be as conservative and accurate as possible when estimating your projected sales figures. Support these projections with evidence, statistics, and as much factual operating data as possible. Also present a detailed cash-flow section that lists biweekly cash-flow projections. Again, this will tie into your sales projections. This section may need to be extensive, especially if you want to show a potential investor your cash-flow growth over a period of, say, six months to a year.

The idea here is to show investors when and how frequently cash will come into the business. It will also give you a projection of your company's progress over the first year.

Another part of this section is the one-year budget. This is your first year's operating budget, including your fixed costs, overhead, salaries, taxes, advertising payments, lease payments, and so on. Variable costs will be incurred after your start-up and may add or decrease your budgeted expenditures. When examining the revenue side of your budget, be conservative.

Be sure to include a breakeven analysis that forecasts what your revenues need to be to cover all your expenses (which may or may not include a salary for you). Keep in mind that the first question after reaching breakeven is, "When will we see a profit?" The purpose of a business is to make money, and lenders and investors will want you to estimate in as much detail as possible when profitability will come and what will get you there.

A final statement on your accounting methods and credit policy will round this section out, and again, if you don't have the finance knowledge to do all elements of this process yourself, by all means enlist a CPA or experienced finance expert as you're constructing the plan.

In particular, your readers are going to want a sense of how you're going to handle bad times. What kinds of credit will you extend to customers and what will be your policies on bad debts, collections, and discounts? Tough economies bring out tough financial questions.

Day-to-Day Operations

The section on day-to-day operations describes staffing plans, training, and other personnel-related issues. If you plan to hire employees, you need to explain how you'll use your people, what they'll cost in pay and benefits, and what value they'll bring to the enterprise. It will also help to explain how you'll scale employment up or down in case business is better or worse than expected.

This section also talks about business support activities such as advertising and marketing. It discusses your market, competition, and methods of pricing. You need to discuss your closest competitors in more detail than you've offered in the industry analysis, as well as the immediate market for your product or service. You're providing a ground-level view of the way you will operate the business each day.

QUICK Tip

Don't Cram: Maybe you were the king or queen of college term papers at the eleventh hour, but a business plan isn't a term paper. It's a living, breathing document that details the most important of all things—your future. Give it the time it needs. Write a draft, and put it down for a few days. Come back to it fresh. With each pass, it will get better, and most important, it will tell you things about yourself and your business idea that you never realized before.

Financing Needs

You may or may not need to ask for money at start-up. But it's wise to complete this section even if it works out that you don't. Why? Because it always costs money to start a business and even more to grow it.

What do we mean? Maybe you're starting a consulting business on your laptop, but you had to buy that laptop, right? And you need to pay for the space and utilities you're operating your business in, correct (even if it's in your attic)? If your revenues grow by a certain percentage by the end of the year, what will your costs be then? Will you need to hire someone to help you?

Catching on?

Writing this section will help you set key performance targets for your business and determine whether or not you'll need funding to help you meet those targets or aim for new ones. It also will help you see—and justify—what your business idea is worth and what you think it will be worth to others.

You've explained your industry, your business concept, your personal and business finances, and your expectations for turning a profit on this great idea you had. You have made a solid, logical, and attractive case. Now you're going to offer a number to lenders and investors and hope they bite.

Now it's time to reel them in.

QUICK Tip

Asking Questions: No question is stupid. Every industry has its own financial structure and conventions and every group of funders has its own set of standards for lending money or making an investment. Your "ask" has to be tailored to them, not the other way around.

Summary

Consider this section the bookend to the executive summary at the front of your business plan. You've probably taken the shortcut in reading a report by turning to the summary page yourself and you know what this is—it's a page or two devoted to reinforcing to people the most important stuff you've already told them.

How should you write it? Again, refer to other business plans you've collected that are common to your industry, but like the executive summary, you're working to save people time. Do it here by using bullet points to summarize the top one to three points from each section.

Appendix

In this section, show any supporting documents, charts, or indexes you have to support your plan for the specific audience, as well as information about your proposed board of directors.

It's important to know that this book gives only a very general overview of what you should include in your business plan. We recommend several books in chapter 13 that will help you compose this important document in detail. If you can get your hands on successful business plans in your industry by networking or by checking libraries at business schools, that might also help you craft the style for a successful plan.

Never be scared to ask what specific readers want to see in a business plan as part of their review process. Ask them if they have a plan they thought was particularly well constructed and if they will share it with you (after clearing it with the author, of course).

Over time, you may want to revise your plan periodically or write a new two- to five-year plan. This will include many items pertaining to the future of your business, including your growth rates and goals after your first year of operation. Chapter 12 includes an entire section on strategic planning, the follow-up to writing a business plan.

The Seven Main Types of Business Entities

- ▶ **Sole proprietorship**

- ▶ **General partnership**

- ▶ **Limited partnership**

- ▶ **Limited liability company (LLC)**

- ▶ **Limited liability partnership (LLP)**

- ▶ **Corporation (C corporation)**

- ▶ **Subchapter S corporation (S corporation)**

The business entity you choose is important for structural, liability, and tax reasons. As already mentioned, the type of entity is among the first decisions you'll make in starting your business. The entrepreneur may choose from simple forms like sole proprietorships or complex ones like subchapter S corporations.

Each entity is designed for different business needs, and every type of business fits into one of the seven main entity types, as shown in figure 5.1. Also, SOHOs must select an entity as well.

Figure 5.1: BUSINESS ENTITY SELECTION LIST

The numerous types of business entities are listed here. Overall, the options include the following:

- **Sole proprietorship**

- **General partnership**

- **Limited partnership**

- **Limited liability company**

- **Limited liability partnership**

- **Corporation (C corporation)**

- **Subchapter S corporation (S corporation)**

In addition, all states have nonprofit corporations and some have other forms of nonprofit entities. Nonprofit is usually for a charitable organization or a similar entity, and these are not usually what we classify as a "business" that someone would be interested in starting. For information on these, contact a lawyer.

QUICK Tip

Talking with Experts: If you're doing a start-up, it's definitely wise to speak with a lawyer and an accountant, but this step becomes crucial if you're buying an existing business. The business operating entity you select depends on two main issues: your personal financial, tax, and liability circumstances, and the financial, tax, and liability circumstances specific to the type of business you will be operating. Even if you already have specific training in the law or finance, it's almost always better to get qualified representation in these matters, if only for the sounding board.

In this chapter, we provide a synopsis of the main for-profit forms of companies with the strengths and weaknesses of each entity. Again, we don't intend to take the place of a qualified adviser in these matters, so our descriptions are purposely generic—the business entity you choose must fit your personal and business goals specifically.

Also, remember that each state defines these entities in its own specific way. In chapter 14, we provide links to forms and agencies that can help you define these categories, as well as state-specific contacts for lawyers, certified public accountants, and qualified local business advisers if you need them.

But as a starting point, take a look at figure 5.2 for the questions you'll have to answer in determining your entity. Then ask your advisers to help you zero in on your final choice.

Figure 5.2: BUSINESS ENTITY SELECTION LIST

Some specific things to consider when selecting an entity type are the following:

1. Liability needs

How much protection from the company's actions do you personally require? Does your form of business generally require liability protection?

Continued

2. Capital and financial requirements
How much capital do you have, and how much will you need over the next few years? How easily can you raise that capital under each type of entity?

3. Size
How big are you now, and how big do you plan to become? What entity fits your business size?

4. The business you are in
Certain businesses are best run under certain entity types. Does your business work best under a certain type?

5. Scope of your business operation
Are you doing business locally, statewide, or across state boundaries? What type of entity makes your business operation run best?

6. Short- and long-term goals
What are your goals? How does each entity facilitate the fulfillment of those goals?

The following sections summarize the primary business entities you'll have to work with in all fifty states and the District of Columbia.

Sole Proprietorship

This is the simplest and most common form of business in America. As of 2008, the U.S. Census reported 22.6 million sole proprietors throughout the nation, particularly with the surge in home-based businesses in recent years.

Sole proprietors choose that status because they don't need the complex liability protection or other features that a corporation or other more complex business entity would offer. Registrations and forms are minor. At most, sole proprietors might need a local business license and must follow certain withholding requirements specific to the city or state they operate in.

Operating a sole proprietorship removes many of the burdensome

QUICK Tip

Working at Home: Thinking of working at home? You've got plenty of company. The number of self-employed individuals who work exclusively from home increased from 3.47 million in 1999 to 4.34 million in 2005, according to the U.S. Census. The total population of those working from home at least part-time increased from 9.48 million to 11.33 million during the same period.

government regulations from day-to-day considerations. Usually, the most intrusive thing is your yearly income taxes. It is you against the world, but not against a Goliath of government red tape. However, you must abide by any regulations that do affect you, so be aware of that.

Those with limited funds and limited goals (at least initially) may choose to become a sole proprietor first. Incorporation or partnership can wait until the company expands. That's not to say that all SOHO or microbusinesses are sole proprietors. If you need the liability protection, go with the corporation, the limited partnership, or the limited liability company.

QUICK Tip

Business Liability: A more complicated business entity doesn't protect you from all potential business liability issues. Talk to an insurance expert about your particular business to make sure.

Here we list some of the pros and cons of this simple yet effective business entity. You may come up with more relative to your business situation.

Pros
- Income is taxed as personal income; you get all the profits and avoid complex tax form filings.
- Easy to start: less paperwork to start it up and keep it running.
- No Employer Identification Number (EIN) required; taxes can be filed via Social Security Number.
- No legal help is needed to start it.

- Low start-up cost and often low operating costs.
- Many sole proprietors are SOHO operators.
- Great for part-time businesses.

Cons
- You are personally liable for all business debts.
- You have unlimited legal liability.
- You'll be buying health insurance and other benefits as a sole proprietor, which may be more expensive on a per-person basis.
- Fund-raising options are limited.
- The business typically ceases to exist with the death of the proprietor.

General Partnership

In a general partnership, two or more people create a for-profit, unincorporated business and are equal owners and stewards of that business. In some ways, general partnerships act like a dual or multiperson sole proprietorship. Partners in this structure share duties, responsibilities, revenue, and liabilities equally.

Partnerships are affected by creating a partnership agreement, which is a simple contract between two or more people. It contains certain information that clarifies what the partnership is about: the partners, the responsibilities of each, the duration, the management, and financial arrangements.

Pros
- Simple to start.
- As in sole proprietorships, income is taxed as personal income.
- Little regulation and few start-up requirements.
- Good for simple businesses or short-term business situations.
- Potentially unlimited duration, with the possibility of partnership being passed to heirs upon the death or incapacity of the original partner.
- Somewhat easier to raise capital in a partnership than a sole proprietorship.

Cons
- No liability protection for the partners.
- The partners may eventually end up doing unequal amounts of the work.

- Partnerships can lead to personal troubles between the partners.
- Actions of one partner bind all partners to the business.
- If you need large amounts of capital or large businesses, you may want to become a corporation instead.
- Partnership ends when one owner dies or leaves the company, unless the agreement is written to name successor partners.

Limited Partnership

Limited partnerships include two types of partners: general partners who assume a leadership role and limited partners who are limited in their liability to the amount they initially invested in the partnership.

This form of business functions the same way as a general partnership does, with one exception. The limited partnership is often required to register with the state government. Usually, a form is filled out and sent to the state for approval.

A partnership might choose to become a limited partnership depending on certain factors. Foremost is the desire of one partner to supply capital but not effort. That would be the limited partner. The remaining general partner(s) would be responsible for day-to-day operations and would assume the partnership's liability.

If you do not wish to become a corporation or limited liability company but need to protect the liability of your investing partners, the limited partnership is for you. Limited partnerships have more regulations and usually require state licensing, which sets them apart from general partnerships. Consult chapter 14 for resources to learn more about your state's limited partnership requirements.

Pros

- The limited partners have liability protection.
- Income is taxed as personal income only.
- Potentially unlimited duration.
- Good way to raise capital through limited partners.
- Little government regulation.

Cons

- General partners have maximum liability exposure and do all of the work.
- Limited partners can take their investment out of the company.

- Partners leaving the firm will generally have to be bought out on the basis of a negotiated share price.
- Disputes can be costly if dissolution plans are not clear from the beginning.

Limited Liability Company (LLC)

Limited liability companies (LLCs) are comparatively newer business entities that are hybrids of limited partnerships and corporations. Limited liability companies feature ease of formation, tax savings, and liability protection. These are fast becoming a very popular business election.

Basically, LLCs are companies with corporate liability protection and stockholding capabilities, and they are taxed only once at the ownership level. (Double taxation occurs on the corporate level.) Recent laws have enabled LLCs to obtain almost the same liability and tax protections as S corporations, which we'll get to in a moment, without certain corporation requirements and regulations. For small businesses that desire most of the benefits of incorporation, this is the way to go.

Pros

- Income is taxed only once, similar to sole proprietorships.
- Can have more than one class of stock.
- Has unlimited liability protection, like corporations.

Cons

- Still not a corporation with the credibility offered by the *Inc.* at the end of the business name, which can be a turnoff for lenders and investors.
- Potential limitation on years of operation, depending on state rules.
- May or may not be the right choice of entity depending on business and personal finance situation—it's very important to vet the decision with lawyers and accountants.

Becoming a limited liability company usually requires filing certain forms, much along the lines of a corporation. However, it can usually be done easily. Be sure to study your particular state's requirements before making the election.

Limited Liability Partnership (LLP)

Limited liability partnerships (LLPs) are very similar to LLCs. The difference is that an LLP is a partnership with protection afforded to the partners as one. As such, it does not offer the incentive of raising capital through stock. Most small businesspeople don't use this election, but if you do, a section is listed in the next chapter on how to do it. Refer to the LLC section for pros and cons.

Corporation (C Corporation)

The corporation (C corporation) is your plain-vanilla corporate entity. A corporation is a for-profit organization created under the auspices of your state government. It is incorporated to do business within your state by an act of your state government. Millions of corporations dot the business landscape.

A corporation is owned by one or more people, called stockholders, but stockholders are separate from the company itself. This means that stockholders have unlimited liability protection from the actions of the corporation. They cannot be held responsible for the actions of the corporation. That onus falls on the company executives and the company itself. Be aware of this fact before you make any decisions. The corporation offers legal protection for its owners, as they are separated from the company.

Because it is licensed to operate by state charter, the corporation is more regulated than most other forms of business entities. Start-up requirements usually include forms, fees, and stock certificates. However, the corporation offers distinct advantages, including better capital generation, stock, liability protection, unlimited life, and a professional name.

And because of state recognition, the corporate *Inc.* at the end of a name may be a psychological aid in company credibility with future lenders and investors. Many companies are incorporated in certain states for tax, regulation, and financial reasons. Small companies are probably better off sticking with registration requirements in their own state.

Pros

• Unlimited liability protection for stockholders.
• Can offer more than one class of stock.

- The *Inc.* name may add credibility and professionalism to a business name and make an organization more attractive to investors and lenders who can help raise capital.
- Hierarchy and structure may make duties within the corporation easier to define for partners starting a business.

Cons

- Income is taxed at the corporate and stockholder level.
- Many ongoing state regulations and yearly requirements.
- To do business in another state, you must file foreign corporation registrations with that state.
- Company subjected to desires of a board of directors that represents the stockholders.
- Start-up is more lengthy and expensive than other elections.
- The election is accomplished by filing certain forms with your secretary of state. In addition, yearly or biyearly requirements include such things as annual reports. Your state requirements will vary.
- Most large companies are corporations primarily for the liability protection. You will make your election depending on your needs. However, you will want to at least investigate limited liability companies and S corporations before making the regular corporation election. Either of the former will probably save you a great deal in taxes.

Subchapter S Corporation (S Corporation)

Subchapter S corporations were created to give the owners of the corporation all the benefits (including limited liability) of the regular corporation, but without high corporate taxes. Both LLCs and S corporations are similar, but they are not the same: both allow income to be "passed through" to the owners of the company, thus avoiding the double taxation issues associated with corporations.

Generally, S corporations are losing favor in some small business circles because they tend to involve more bureaucracy—setting up a formal board of directors, filing annual reports, and so on—whereas LLCs do not have many of those requirements.

The S corporation election is made by filing Form 2553 with the IRS. The S corporation can have seventy-five or fewer American stockholders who hold one class of stock. It allows for the transfer of stock to family members and includes the prime incentive of single taxation on all company income.

Ongoing changes in tax and regulatory laws affect all business entities, especially S corporations and limited liability companies. Keep abreast of current rules and regulations. They may have changed since publication.

Pros

- Stockholders have liability protection for the actions of the company.
- Income is taxed only once at the shareholder level.
- Growth and raising capital is easier than certain other entity types.
- Losses can be used to offset personal income.
- Is basically a corporation but with better tax structure.

Cons

- Has only one class of stock.
- Has many start-up requirements, including more federal requirements and potential state requirements.
- May be under more IRS scrutiny.
- Must adhere to strict fiscal and state guidelines.

Business entities can be changed as companies grow. But as part of your business plan, you've hopefully gotten an idea of how you'll handle national or global expansion. Where you want to do business is a critical issue that you need to consider at the organizational stage of the business.

If you need to do business in another state, have your lawyer check the other state's laws first and file any applicable forms. You can do this yourself, but you may, at this stage in your growth, want to get a lawyer to make sure all requirements are met and to allow you to concentrate on running your business and making money.

These business entity types will no doubt change over the course of the years to come, but for now, these are the main types. Remember to carefully consider your election. This will affect your company for the next several years. Later, you can always become a different business entity, but you must check the rules and regulations before you do so.

Chapter

6

The Basics of Forming Each Type of Business Entity

▶ **Taking one last look before you leap**

▶ **Forming your business entity**

▶ **Setting up the seven entities in detail**

SOLE PROPRIETORSHIP

GENERAL PARTNERSHIP

LIMITED PARTNERSHIP

LIMITED LIABILITY COMPANY

LIMITED LIABILITY PARTNERSHIP

CORPORATION

SUBCHAPTER S CORPORATION

By now, you should have a pretty good idea of the business entity you will use to structure your company. You answered the essential start-up questions, and you wrote a great business plan.

Now you can begin the process of actually starting the business. But it's a good idea to check your steps once again.

Taking One Last Look before You Leap

So are you ready? That is, is everything in order, and are you finally prepared to begin the actual work of your small business? If you're starting fresh, are you ready to put in the hours? If you're already doing it part-time, are you ready for the full transition?

Let's review some of the steps you should have taken up to this point.

Is your family on board? You should consider spouses, partners, parents, and children in any decision to start a business. If they are worried or insecure about your move, it's not going to make life easy at home. Work on this first.

Have your finances in the best shape possible. The old saying is "Necessity is the mother of invention," and there's no question that many new businesses are formed when people are out of work or hoping to build their income. But it's particularly important to take a thorough (and independent, if possible) look at your personal finances before you take this risk. Evaluate your level of debt, your expenses, your retirement and health benefits (you'll be paying for these now without the help of an employer), and savings and investments before you take this step.

Would it make sense to work in your target industry first? One of the best ways to understand the particular risks, rewards, and stresses of a particular business is to get experience working for another company before you try it on your own. This is particularly true for retailers and restaurants—businesses that involve constant contact with the public and an unexpectedly high level of physical work. Apprenticeship can be the best entrepreneurial training starting out, so before you leap, consider a full- or part-time post in your target industry before you take on all that risk yourself.

Consider your desired ending for the business. As we stated before, too many people jump into business without a set of goals that will determine whether they will close, sell, pass down, or continue the business. Being in business can be exhausting. You may get so involved in the day to day that you fail to plan for the future. That's why it makes sense to do it now.

QUICK Tip

Getting Good Personal Finance Advice: This book isn't a financial planning guide, but we can't stress enough that personal financial planning is a critical step in planning a business. Stepping out on your own often means a disruption of income and a new world in which you are negotiating your own benefits while trying to ensure a safe retirement. It's a good idea to meet with a financial planner while you're talking to attorneys and accountants about your business picture—the planner can help you make sure that you have an adequate financial cushion before you start your business. Not sure where to find one? Try the Financial Planning Association's PlannerSearch site at http://www.fpanet.org.

Forming Your Business Entity

In chapter 5, we talked about the specifics of each major business entity. Choosing and filing for one involves many personal steps as well as specific processes, forms, fees, and regulations specific to the state or states in which you plan to operate your business.

Each takes different durations of time to form—chapter 14 is your gateway to finding the forms you need but also the expertise to guide you to the right ones, and you'll find links to each state's bar and CPA societies to assist you in that search.

This chapter examines the requirements for each and just what it is like to go through the process. At this point, you might want to study figure 6.1 to brush up on the basic components of business start-up and entity election.

QUICK Tip

Do It Yourself: While many people use lawyers to incorporate, you may do it yourself. Also, a number of resources exist in the form of private companies and publications that show you how to incorporate yourself. Several are listed in chapter 13. The pros of incorporating yourself are primarily in the area of cost—you'll save hundreds and potentially thousands of dollars in lawyers' fees. The cons include the time you'll have to spend developing a learning curve in these matters. It's important to price your time correctly.

QUICK Tip

State Requirements: For entities like corporations, partnerships, and limited liability companies, the requirements vary by state. Some states have more requirements than others and charge more in the way of fees and taxes. By requesting and then reading literature from your secretary of state, you can better decide—with your lawyer, accountant, partner, SCORE officer, and/or your work from this book—what the best entity is for you. Spend some time with figure 6.1, which lists the types of things all business owners, regardless of entity type, need to consider.

Alert!

Choose Wisely: When starting a business, never go with the cheapest and easiest route simply for those reasons. If you need the legal protection of a limited liability company or even that of a corporation, go that route. Likewise, if you are starting a simple SOHO, you may be able to get away with being a sole proprietor or general partnership. Depending on your needs, you should enter into whatever form best suits your business. Our last advice here is, again, to be thorough in your selection process.

Figure 6.1: **ENTITY START-UP TIPS**

The following start-up tips are for all businesses at start-up and after. They are intended to save you money or time. Glance through to see which apply to you.

1. You will most likely need to file Form SS-4 Federal Employer Identification Number with the IRS. You can do this while you are forming your company. A sole proprietor may not need one of these. Consult your accountant, CPA, or the IRS for further information.

2. Prepare your data in advance so they are handy for the lawyer, if one is filing your business entity papers for you. Include all relevant data, including company name and address, your name and address, the number and type of shares available, the purpose of the business, and the duration (usually perpetual).

3. You can save on Form W-2s and the like by getting them directly from the IRS website (http://www.irs.gov). Although they will probably give you only half a dozen, many small businesses do not need more than that, at least for the first year. After that, buy them in bulk at an office supply store.

4. Attend business workshops, seminars, and expositions in your area or state on a regular basis, before and after start-up. They can be invaluable for discovering business information, products, suppliers, and people.

5. Continuing education classes for adults at local, state, or community colleges or at technical schools can help you, partners, or employees learn current practices or brush up on past knowledge. Often, you do not need a previous college degree to attend.

6. Always keep records for at least five to eight years, and keep your start-up records forever. We suggest, however, that you keep all of your records permanently—digitize them if that's an option. It's not just about the threat of audits or lawsuits—having findable records can help you guide your business going forward.

7. Remember, you can change your entity status later if you get larger or your needs change.

Continued

8. For a professional look, no matter what business you'll start, use letter-head, business cards, and professional appearances in your business dealings. Sloth turns off customers and investors.

9. Check with local authorities for licenses and zoning information.

Setting Up the Seven Entities in Detail

For a detailed description of numerous start-up considerations, review figure 6.2. With that said, let's examine how to start each of the seven entity types.

Sole Proprietorship

For a sole proprietorship, all you need to do is become the business. You do not need to fill out legal forms of incorporation. There is no sole proprietor equivalent to the Articles of Incorporation or General Partnership Articles. However, there are certain state and local licensing documents and forms that you may have to complete depending on the kind of business you're trying to create.

If these forms are required, you'll find them at your county recorder's office or applicable county or municipal office. Usually, this will be a business license, a required doing-business-as recording, or local licensing obligations. Other licenses may be required from your state for certain business activities or professions. You should contact the state to inquire about required state forms and/or professional or other licenses. You may need to file tax forms for withholding and sales tax. Again, you'll know if you need to file those.

We suggest that you go through the nine-step process described in chapter 2 just as you would for a partnership or corporation. In fact, you will need to do so to complete your business plan and set up the financial arrangements for your business. You probably will need a sales tax identification number for retail and Employer Identification Number as well, although many sole proprietors get by using their Social Security Numbers.

Once you have set up your business, you can get an account at a bank for checking and other activities. Some owners of very small businesses can simply use their own checking accounts, but we advise looking into a business account.

One final note: for most people, including many SOHO businesses, a sole proprietorship is the way to go, but remember that you have all liability on your shoulders, including financial and legal. Still, this is the easiest and best route for most small businesses. You can always incorporate later, as your company grows.

General Partnership

Like the sole proprietor, the general partnership is easy to enter into. Once again, you simply become the partnership. You and your partner will be general partners, each assuming a share of the risk and return and a share of the duties.

An oral agreement is all that is technically needed to establish a general partnership, but a written agreement is practical, smart, and the best way to go. This way, you and your partner both agree to exactly the same terms, and your signatures make it a contract. Be as concise and exact as possible as a safeguard against possible problems later on. Include the partnership name, the partners, the responsibilities of each, the duration of the partnership, the management and financial arrangements, as well as any special sections that you feel are necessary.

Include complete details about each partner's duties and responsibilities. You might want to bullet them to make them stand out on the agreement. Have the agreement signatures notarized, and each person should keep an original copy of the instrument. If you have any questions, plunk down some money and talk with a lawyer about what to put into the agreement. Still, this is a basic form of business, and you shouldn't have to see a lawyer. Just be concise and thorough in your partnership agreement.

Once you have your partnership agreement, file for a business license with your county recorder's office, if that's required. Make sure that you have any and all licenses needed. Check your local and state governments for these. After this, you can set up your checking account at a local bank. It is prudent to leave the responsibility of finances to just one of the partners, and this should be noted as part of the partnership agreement. However, both partners should be able to utilize checking accounts connected with the business.

Remember, a periodic review of your partnership agreement and your business plan will ensure that your partnership is on the right track.

Limited Partnership

The limited partnership starts the more complex start-up entities, although the processes are all very easy. Here, you have one or more general partners and one or more limited partners. States regulate limited partnerships more closely than general partnerships or sole proprietors. Thus, it is a good idea to contact your state for more information (e.g., forms, rules, codes) before talking to a lawyer.

To form a limited partnership, create and write a partnership agreement that clearly enumerates the same things for a general partnership as we listed in the previous section and the role in the partnership of the limited partner(s).

Most states will require you to file a form called a limited partnership certificate or a certificate of limited partnership. Get this from a lawyer or the state (again, check chapter 14 for the contact information and key web addresses), file it with the appropriate fee, and wait for the return certificate. Some states may require your partnership agreement to be submitted with their forms.

Next, you will generally file for a business license at your county recorder or clerk's office and apply for any other necessary state licenses. After this, you can set up your checking account at a local bank. Again, it is prudent to leave the finances to one of the partners, and this should be noted as part of the partnership agreement.

Limited Liability Company

The LLC is set up in a similar fashion as the corporation. Once ready, simply set up your structure of partners, investors, and officers. File the certificate of limited liability organization (name may vary), consent (certificate) of registered agent, and any trade-name registration needed.

These forms are filed with your secretary of state. Others may be necessary depending on your state requirements. The fees vary by state but are generally not too expensive.

Usually, you will list the name of the company, the address, the name and address of the registered agent, the date the company is to dissolve, the names of the organizers or managers, and the rights the company will have. This is a vague template that your state may or may not follow. It is signed by the organizers and dated. The words *limited liability company* or *LLC* usually must be included in your company name.

When you write to your state to request forms, you will be given a list of fees and forms to file. Once these forms are submitted, you will receive a certification and can get your bank account, as well as your business license at your county recorder's office. Again, be sure to check with your state or lawyer for any other licenses particular to your business or industry.

Limited Liability Partnership

The LLP is similar to the company, except it is a partnership. Where it exists, this entity is elected by filing the limited liability partnership certificate or selection. Again, there may not be a standard form for this, and you may have to create it yourself. Not all states have this election, so write to your state for more information. Generally, *LLP* or *Limited Liability Partnership* must appear in the name. After you start an LLP, though, you can get your bank account, your county business license, and any other licenses.

Corporation

Incorporating is similar in process to forming a limited liability company, except most states have a simple one- or two-page form that you must fill out and submit. You can, under most circumstances, write your own articles if you wish to include more information than is included on the form. For most business start-ups, the form that comes from the state will be enough. Most states have separate forms for regular and professional corporations.

Usually, your state form will ask you for the name of the corporation; the incorporators; the registered agent; the initial number of stock shares, their value, and their type; your duration (usually forever); the original company officers; and the purpose of your incorporation (what you are going to do).

Generally, if you are doing this yourself, you will first reserve a trade name, register your agent, and file the articles of incorporation. The state will return the forms as filed and you can start business. You will need a corporate minutes book with stock certificates showing your initial shares and the value—use simple forms or go to an office stationery store for these. A shareholder's meeting must be held after you incorporate to elect officers of your board. That board must then meet for the first time to select bylaws. Since it is your company, you will most likely have the minutes and stock shares, so your first meeting should be quite easy. Remember to document the meeting, though; you are now a business and should conduct affairs accordingly.

QUICK Tip

Remember to Verify: The business entity selection conversation throughout this chapter outlines the typical start-up requirements for most states. States vary, so use chapter 14 to connect with your state's guidelines or work through a trusted attorney or accountant to make sure you make the right choice.

These are generalized guidelines but are usually true for most states. Study your state's websites and contact them if you have questions on various requirements.

Your signatures will be required on many of the forms. If more information is needed, your lawyer may write an article of incorporation him- or herself to include much more information that is pertinent to your wishes and your company's goals. The attorney will handle most of the requirements for you, but make sure to get in writing what services he or she will perform for what fee.

The minimum is filing for a reserved name, filing your articles of incorporation, getting stock certificates, creating bylaws, and filing your federal identification numbers. Simply ask the attorney what the fee encompasses. Either way, you fill out, sign, and send your incorporation forms to the state.

You will also write your bylaws, as mentioned earlier. These are the codes, rules, and regulations used in day-to-day operations—no matter the size of the company.

Often, a lawyer can do this for you in lieu of an initial stockholders' meeting or can assist you in writing the bylaws. Operating under standard business codes, the requirements are straightforward and are designed to keep your business running in a professional manner in compliance with laws and codes. These bylaws must be registered with the secretary of state.

Finally, professional business licenses from the state or state boards are usually required. You'll need to make sure that you know whether your business—or you personally—needs to be licensed or bonded.

Subchapter S Corporation

For a subchapter S corporation, you will file your forms generally as described earlier—again, get in contact with your state's agencies and advisory resources through chapter 14. Generally, the only real difference is that you or your lawyer must file Form 2553 with the IRS.

After this, your only differences come in the number of stockholders and the annual tax returns. The S corporation is required to file income tax returns, but all income is taxed at the shareholder level.

Figure 6.2: SPECIAL NOTES FOR START-UP BUSINESSES

- The address for the company can be your home if you follow zoning and IRS codes. Your home office should not be a place where customers come, unless you are zoned for business as well as residential.

- Any additional local or special state fees may also be required with regulatory licenses. To incorporate, a lawyer will cost between $400 and $1,000, but usually around $500. Tax number fees can cost more, as can other fees (incorporation, limited partnership, and stock fees).

- If you choose to go the self-incorporation route, you can obtain forms from your state or from books or online services that offer such assistance. In most cases, however, it's important to get help on the ground from qualified attorneys.

- For many entity types, franchise taxes, initial annual reports, securities filings, and Uniform Commercial Code filings may be required. These vary greatly from state to state. It's important to research every aspect of your state's requirements. Check chapter 13 for more information.

- Remember that you are usually required to hold a board of directors meeting at least annually and to submit annual or biennial reports if you are a corporation or limited liability company. Again, know your state's requirements.

- For certain larger start-ups, avoiding lawyers will be extremely difficult for most people. They do, after all, handle incorporations all the time and will answer your questions. Most novice incorporators have dozens of questions, and good lawyers will be patient with you and answer them. Do try and consolidate questions and work matters to make the best use of their time and your money.

Chapter 7

Franchising: The Alternative

- ▶ **The pros and cons of franchising**
- ▶ **How the best franchises operate**
- ▶ **Risks and returns**
- ▶ **Networking is important**
- ▶ **Understanding the financing**

At this point in the book, it is worthwhile to discuss franchising as an option for owning your own small business. You may be interested in buying a franchise, or you may eventually franchise your own business as it grows and becomes successful.

Franchising is a business concept whereby a parent company uses affiliated owners to distribute or sell its products or services. It usually involves the parent company collecting an upfront licensing fee, an annual fee, and a percentage of the profit from the franchisee. In return, the franchisee gets to use the company name and the product or service and participate in the collective advertising of the whole firm. Some franchises allow more leeway in day-to-day operations and planning than others. It all depends on the franchisor and its business practices.

The process of starting up a franchise business can run the financial gamut from modest to costly. Some franchises can be purchased for a few thousand dollars, but these are typically not location franchises but rather business ideas and systems that you run from your home or through mail order. Others are more involved, some costing several hundred thousand dollars to start—so between franchise fees and other required investments, acquiring a single location of a top restaurant franchise can cost upward of $500,000. Many franchises work out deals with potential franchisees to finance the purchase of the franchise. The fees and costs to operate a franchise also vary greatly.

QUICK Tip

Franchises: Franchise businesses were hit hard during the recession of the early 2000s, according to data from the International Franchise Association. After three consecutive years of decline, the organization projected in 2012 that the number of franchises would increase nearly 2 percent by year-end.

Owning a franchise is like owning a small business that's part of a big business. For instance, if you own one Subway sandwich franchise, you run it like a small business, but you are actually part of a giant network of other franchise locations and the corporate headquarters.

The U.S. Commerce Department and the Census Bureau teamed up in 2010 on a comprehensive review of the U.S. franchise industry and found that based on (pre-recession) 2007 statistics, franchise businesses accounted for 10.5 percent of businesses with paid employees in the 295 industries for which franchising data were collected. In addition, franchise businesses accounted for nearly $1.3 trillion of the $7.7 trillion in total sales for these industries, $153.7 billion out of the $1.6 trillion in total payroll, and 7.9 million workers out of a total workforce of 59.0 million. Other facts from the report:

- Limited-service restaurants, sometimes called fast food restaurants, had the highest number of franchise establishments with paid employees (124,898), followed by gas stations with convenience stores (33,991) and full-service restaurants (30,130).
- New car dealers led in sales for franchise establishments ($687.7 billion), followed by gas stations with convenience stores ($131.1 billion) and limited-service restaurants ($112.6 billion).
- Sales for franchise establishments in the diet and weight-loss centers industry represented 62.7 percent of all sales for that industry, ranked third behind new car dealers (100 percent) and limited-service restaurants (74.4 percent).

Everyone knows and uses franchised businesses. Scores of established and commonplace franchises operate across the nation, even in small towns and rural areas.

Yet franchising isn't quite like having a business that's fully under your control. In exchange for an established brand name, which might be the most valuable part of a business, you will be responsible for meeting certain operating standards and performance targets. The franchisor—the company controlling their stable of franchisees—does this to protect the value of its brand and the customer experience associated with it.

The Pros and Cons of Franchising

Franchising may be an option for you if you are unsure about going it "alone" in business. But be aware that this is no easier a route than any of the other options. It takes long hours, a lot of money, and determination for the franchise to succeed. The only difference is the fact that the franchisor is behind you, which may eliminate some of the anxiety and uncertainty associated with starting a business.

Pros

- A business in a box that gives you—the franchisee—the product or service and the inventory and support materials behind it.
- An established brand that you and your potential customers already know.
- Standardized training to run the business.
- Centralized local, national, or international marketing and advertising with a potentially wide reach that you don't have to create.
- An established and most likely successful business network of people doing exactly what you do whom you can share information and experience with.
- An opportunity to expand and make more money based on your success.

Cons

- Potentially high start-up costs that the franchisor may or may not help you finance.
- Potentially high qualifications set by the franchisor to establish their team.
- Heavy legal, financial, and regulatory requirements at start-up.
- The franchisor will decide whether you get to keep or expand your business on the basis of its requirements.
- You must follow the franchisor's pricing, product, and marketing instructions.
- Fees and sales percentages given back to the franchisor can be steep, and on the basis of poor performance and other factors indicated in your agreement, your franchisor can put you out of business and name a new franchisee to take over your franchise and/or location.

The one thing you need to remember about operating a franchise is that it's the franchisor's name on the door, not yours.

Small office and home office franchises exist, and their ads can be found in many small business magazines. Typically, these are low-cost, less profitable franchises. The franchisor may not be able to provide as much technical assistance and marketing prowess as with larger franchises. However, you may be able to start one part-time and then move to full-time. But be wary of anything that sounds too good to be true, especially if you go looking for a part-time SOHO franchise.

A good place to start researching the franchise business is the U.S.

Federal Trade Commission (FTC). Its main website (http://www
.ftc.gov) has a link to the agency's business center where very helpful
and basic information is located, including its "Buying a Franchise: A
Consumer Guide," which is available for download.

How the Best Franchises Operate

Note that we used the word *best* here. Starting your research with the
FTC is a good idea because it prosecutes scams and because some franchisors are simply better than others.

The parent company of a franchise should provide you with a few
basic types of support and assistance. None of these is guaranteed,
however. You must carefully analyze prospective franchises by reading
the literature sent to you and by asking questions of claims and statistics.
It also helps you to seek out legal and accounting experts who have
specific experience working with franchise owners just to get their input
on what you should ask before you approach a franchisor.

If a franchisor does not supply you with everything the FTC and your
advisers encourage you to check for, ask for the missing information. If
there's resistance on the part of the franchisor to supply you with what
you need, be wary.

This is one case where the government is on your side. Also, get
everything in writing. Remember, this is your future, so take the time
to think it out.

Risks and Returns

When you begin contemplating a franchise, it's worth consulting figure 7.1, which covers a series of ways to evaluate the risks and returns
involved in buying a franchise. Consult the Federal Trade Commission's
information as well.

It's also important to check with your statewide offices to see which
rules and regulations might exist for franchise operation closer to home.
Those contacts are in chapter 14.

Two organizations that aid franchisees are the American Association
of Franchisees and Dealers and the International Franchise Association.
These organizations can provide assistance, benefits, and networking
opportunities.

You'll also learn something from national newspapers and magazines tailored to small business audiences. The following offer stories and features about the franchise industry as well as specific advertising for franchise opportunities:

- *Wall Street Journal*
- *USA Today*
- *Entrepreneur* and Entrepreneur.com
- *Franchise Times*
- *Inc.* magazine and Inc.com

QUICK Tip

Getting the News: News articles and advertising are educational, but don't take them as gospel. Major national newspapers and magazines carry advertising from well-known and not-so-well-known franchisors explaining the availability of franchise licenses in a host of industries. Do what you do with all advertising. Check them out for educational value, but don't necessarily believe everything you read. Be prepared to back up your information with your own research.

You can find the addresses, phone numbers, and/or Internet addresses of many of these sources of information on franchising in chapter 13.

Networking Is Important

Also, if you have a franchise in mind, do everything you can to seek out and talk to a current franchisee. As long as you don't plan to open a location in his or her territory, that franchisee can be a great resource of day-to-day operating advice.

When you speak with an attorney and an accountant on a potential franchise opportunity, go over all the background and documents with a fine-toothed comb so you're 100 percent sure of each and every detail.

Evaluate the market, your goals, the franchise, the franchisor's claims, and the franchisor's representatives. Prepare your own business plan based on the one in this book, and be sure to ask yourself every conceivable question before entering into a franchise agreement. The plan will help you evaluate your goals and prepare you for your new business.

Figure 7.1: **FRANCHISE START-UP PRECAUTIONS**

This list is a general guide of considerations to bear in mind when considering franchise opportunities. Again, other publications and books will offer more detailed information, and we urge you to consult them.

- Be aware of the risks. Like any business, there are good franchises and bad franchises. Take the time to find out which is which.

- Protect yourself by self-evaluation. Again, ask yourself whether you can handle the strains—financial, physical, mental—before you franchise.

- Protect yourself by investigating the franchise. Compare and contrast; talk to a variety of franchisors and franchisees.

- Protect yourself by studying disclosure statements. Here, the company should provide you with prospectuses or disclosure statements that contain information of several details of the franchise. Ask for one if they do not give you one. This is important.

- Protect yourself by checking out the disclosures. Field check the information in the disclosures by calling or visiting franchisees.

- Question earnings claims. Some states force franchisors to provide detailed information on this, but some do not. Earnings are the whole point of the business, so be careful.

- Obtain professional advice. This can be from government, industry, or individuals. The only thing that matters is that you do it. Talk to franchisors, franchisees, bankers, business leaders, lawyers, and accountants, just as you would for any other business option.

- Know your legal rights. Discuss these with a lawyer familiar with franchise work.

Understanding the Financing

The next step is to obtain the necessary financing and documentation to start the franchise. The documents vary from company to company, as do the capital requirements.

Again, you will need a lawyer to go over the documents, which vary from franchise to franchise. It is important to remember not to rush into anything. Be aware of all the legal, accounting, tax, financial, and personal responsibilities you will have to yourself, the franchise store, and the parent company.

Franchising can be a wonderful, fulfilling career. It can lead to other businesses. If you are not purchasing a franchise, you might think about franchising your own small business someday. Franchising can also be financially successful for you, if you work at it. Just know the facts first.

Chapter 8

Money: The Root of All Business

Money is the root of all business. This is not some catchy phrase designed to get your attention. No matter what your other motivations are, making money has to rank near the top of the list of reasons to start a small business. If you understand this, you will also clearly understand that start-up capital is one of the most vital parts of launching any business.

A business can't be launched without some amount of capital, even if it's only a few hundred dollars. The amount depends on your needs and your goals. Your business plan will contain this information. It is vital to properly capitalize your small business and to develop resources and methods to obtain further capital. A company without proper financing will have a tough time competing with established competitors. In addition, a lack of capital will raise the risk of your business eventually closing or going bankrupt, neither of which you want. This chapter examines the current environment in business lending and where you should be looking for capital if you can't self-finance.

After the "Great Recession"

Readers of the earliest editions of this book faced a much more favorable lending and funding environment than at this publication. The Thomson Reuters/Paynet Small Business Lending Index is considered a leading indicator of the economy because small businesses generally respond to changes in economic conditions much faster than large companies do. You can find this index through a Google search or on http://www .thomsonreuters.com.

This lending index tells a very interesting seven-year story—and one that indicates that the global economy, which faced the worst economic downturn since the Great Depression, is not out of the woods yet. This climate may make it difficult for you to get a traditional bank loan as you prepare to start your business. Entrepreneurs will have to be very diligent and get very creative about their sources of business capital.

Sources of Business Capital

Basically, capital is money used to run your business. When you start your business, chances are that your first source of capital will probably be your own wallet, savings account, or cashed-in insurance policy.

Using your own savings is the simplest way to get start-up capital.

QUICK Tip

How's Your Credit? We're not talking about business credit. We'll get back to that in a minute. We're talking about *your* credit. We live in an information age, and banks are not the only institutions with access to credit data. Prospective investors can get their hands on this data as well. If you don't check your credit reports from the three primary agencies—Equifax, Transunion, and Experian—on a regular basis, then start. Make sure you're checking for ID theft as well as credit inaccuracies. It's also a very good idea to pay down as much personal debt as you can before you attempt to borrow or accept investment dollars from anyone—you'll look more like someone worth investing in.

People call this bootstrapping. You are the first (and maybe only) person to be interested in investing in this company you are founding. Therefore, you must be prepared to shell out your own hard-earned savings to help your business through its first few months, realizing that you could lose your money. If you are working part-time in your business, you may have income from your regular job that you can use for start-up costs and to help keep you afloat personally.

The following is a basic skeleton of the many places in which you can potentially obtain start-up capital, including loans, friends, partners, venture capitalists, and stock sales.

Loans

Business Loans

The bank is often the first place entrepreneurs think of when it comes to obtaining financing. Even in the best of economies, new companies are rarely a draw for bank lenders, because untested businesses make for risky investments. The willingness to lend money to a start-up business often depends on the policy of the bank and the criteria it has established to loan money. Typically, a bank will loan money to a client only if the client has collateral, has impeccable personal credit qualifications, or can repay the loan with ongoing income from something other than the start-up business.

The criteria banks use to lend money are the amount and purpose of the loan, the primary and secondary sources of repaying the loan, the company data (such as management and operations), the financial data (including balance sheets and cash-flow statements you created for your business plan), your personal credit history, and the reliability of the company. Any loan is usually secured by the equipment, personal or company assets, or the land being purchased. That does not stop most banks from wanting you to have full collateral.

Getting a loan at a bank is difficult; we'll tell you that up front. Most start-ups will not get them. However, if you can grow your business steadily over a period of time, banks will be more inclined to lend you money because you will have proved that you can operate your business successfully. Many small business owners will simply have to grow their businesses first before approaching a bank. Smaller banks might be more apt to loan to a start-up or a SOHO business than a larger bank. Check local small banks for their policies.

So with the odds against you, how do you approach a bank? Present yourself impeccably, be calm, answer questions honestly and directly, and have a killer business plan. Circumlocution, stammering, and lying are not things you want to do in front of the loan officer. Remember, too, that honesty is the best policy. If the first bank turns you down, you can try another bank. Some first-time business start-ups have gone to several banks before getting a loan. Have patience.

If you qualify for a loan, you will want to know a few types of loan products that banks offer. These can vary by bank or by region, but figure 8.1 shows the basics. Loans are typically paid for in installment payments or in balloon payments, which are a combination of installment loans with a final large payment. Some banks offer seasonal credit and bridge loans to cover specific periods in the business year.

It's important to consider that banks want a full relationship with a client. They want you to take advantage of the other services they offer so that they make more money off of you beyond loan interest. These services can include free checking; lines of credit; credit and debit cards; and increasingly, a range of cash management services. They'll also try to gain your personal business. Owners of small businesses should evaluate the advantages of using the same bank for personal and business banking or of using different banks for each.

Figure 8.1: **BANK FINANCING**

Banks can usually offer three general types of financing options. Study up on them before you request financing from a bank. Here are some primary bank offerings:

1. Revolving lines of credit. Here you receive a line of credit payable over the course of, say, a year. Usually these are small amounts between $5,000 and $50,000. You generally can use the credit as you need it and are charged only on what you use.
2. Intermediate term debt. These shorter-term loans are usually sixty months or less in duration, and they are secured by collateral, such as equipment purchased. These are good ways to get equipment.
3. Term loans. These are used to generally acquire real estate and are typically amortized for up to 180-month periods. For small businesses, you will typically see loans up to the $100,000 mark.

Personal Loans

Another option is to get a loan in your name as opposed the business name—in other words, a personal loan. The most popular types of personal loans today are home equity loans and home equity lines of credit, both of which are based on the value of the equity you have in your home. Conventional installment loans are also available at local banks and credit unions of all sizes. While the interest rates are fixed with conventional installment loans, you are generally limited to five years for the length of the loan. Home equity loans, however, can have fixed terms up to thirty years.

Home Equity Loans

The post-2006 real estate collapse has made the option of a home equity loan tougher for many individuals, but taking out a loan on the equity of your home is a common way to tap operating capital for one's business.

Pros

- Not required to explain in detail your new business or business plan to the bank.

- Interest is usually tax deductible; consult with your accountant or tax adviser regarding this potentially money-saving feature.
- Most banks, large and small, offer home equity loans.
- Maturity or length of loan can range between five to thirty years.
- Fixed interest rate for length of loan.

Cons

- A difficult option in a tough consumer lending environment.
- The idea of using your home can make some people nervous about this choice, particularly if it affects your personal finances.
- Limited to the amount of equity in your home; if you have not lived in your home for a long period of time, you may be unable to raise the amount of money you need from this source alone.
- Some fees are involved, such as an appraisal to determine the value of your home and therefore the equity available.

Home Equity Line of Credit

Although a home equity line of credit provides many of the same advantages home equity loans do, they are different in a few important ways. First, the interest rate is not fixed and will change as market interest rates move up or down over time. They are usually pegged at a predetermined spread to the prime lending rate. Second, with a line of credit, you pay interest only on the amount of money you use, not on the full line amount you have been approved for by the bank.

Pros

- Home equity lines of credit are now a common category of consumer credit.
- You are not required to explain in detail your new business or business plan to the bank.
- Interest is usually tax deductible; consult with your accountant or tax adviser regarding this potentially money-saving feature.
- Most banks, large and small, offer home equity lines of credit.
- Pay interest only on the amount you use.
- Many banks now offer an online application process.
- Variable interest rate, usually tied to the prime lending rate.

Cons

- Using your home as collateral for the loan.
- Limited to the amount of equity in your home; if you have not lived in your home for a long period of time, you may be unable to raise the amount of money you need from this source alone.
- Some fees are involved, such as an appraisal to determine the value of your home and therefore the equity available.

Personal Installment Loans

Personal installment loans may be used in conjunction with other types or sources of capital-generating techniques. Since these loans are usually for more modest amounts of money and are usually required to be repaid within five years, other sources of capital will likely be required.

Pros

- Usually easier to obtain than a small business loan.
- You are not required to explain in detail your new business or business plan to the bank.
- Can use cars, boats, certificates of deposit, stocks, or other personal assets as collateral.
- Available at all banks and credit unions.
- Online application process available at most banks.
- Fixed interest rate on loan.

Cons

- Limited borrowing ability.
- Generally, these loans have higher interest rates.
- Interest is not tax deductible.

Networking

Friends and Family

A small business often can raise money through friends and family, especially at start-up through investments or loans. Again, you should treat these people with professionalism by explaining the potential risks and returns.

When family and friends invest, they can be lenders, original stockholders, or limited partners. Also, when you need more money or when you issue a direct public offering, they will be the first people you contact. If you run a SOHO business, this is an excellent source of start-up funds. Friends and family will be more likely to back you in one of these ventures than capitalists, the SBA, or bankers.

Another take on this source of financing is to tap into business colleagues or other businesspeople you may know, work with, or have networked with in the past.

Business Partners

Taking in additional business partners either in the form of fellow incorporators or limited partners is another method of raising capital. Often, investors will agree to become a limited partner on the strength of your plan and their faith in your future success. In this situation, your partner is strictly a financial backer. He or she will want to see a return on investment but will not want to participate in any of the work of the company.

This can be an ideal situation if you do not want to sell stock or incorporate and if you have some backers already. Finding limited partners can be difficult, though, if you have to search for them. The laws of your state may not permit advertising, so you will have to network to find them. Often, these will be friends, family members, business associates, college friends, or others who have a professional or personal connection to you or any other principals in your company.

Business Networking and Brand Name Sharing

With business networking, or brand name sharing, one or more business-es combine to share one brand name, although each produces different goods. For example, let's say a group of automotive suppliers cannot get its own brand of products on store shelves because the products are not as well known as other brands. The group signs an agreement, puts the common brand and logo on all products, and uses a combined marketing and distribution system to place the goods. This really works and can increase each participating company's market share dramatically.

Although this method is not capital per se, it is a way to get more out of your capital dollars and a way to raise your market share and product awareness. It is also a way to increase cash flow and revenue, which is one of the prime ways to attract traditional bank and SBA loans.

The Government

U.S. Small Business Administration

The federal government has a variety of departments and programs to aid small businesses, most notably through the U.S. Small Business Administration. In addition, as we mentioned earlier, it has some programs to aid minority- and women-owned small businesses. In addition to loans, the SBA offers assistance in writing a business plan, financial accounting, management, manufacturing, retail, taxes, and other areas.

The SBA operates a multitier loan program for small business. Since the purpose of the SBA is to promote small businesses, it uses the loan program for that end. As of 2012, the SBA had a portfolio of $25.2 billion in loans through the following programs:

• The Microloan Program provides small, short-term loans to small business concerns and certain types of not-for-profit child-care centers. The SBA makes funds available to specially designated intermediary lenders, which are nonprofit.
• The 7(a) Loan Program is the SBA's primary program to help start-up and existing small businesses obtain financing when they might not be eligible for business loans through normal lending channels.
• The Certified Development Company/504 loan program is a long-term financing tool, designed to encourage economic development within a community. The 504 Program accomplishes this by providing small businesses with long-term, fixed-rate financing to acquire major fixed assets for expansion or modification.
• Guaranteed Loan Programs (Debt Financing) enable banks and other lending institutions to offer a number of SBA guaranteed loan programs to assist small businesses. Although the SBA itself does not make loans, it does guarantee loans made to small businesses by private and other institutions.

Grants and Incentives

Sometimes foundations and government sources offer grants and incentives to small businesses. Local governments sometimes offer utility rate and property tax incentives for small businesses that employ locals. Many cities have community development corporations (CDCs), which are charged with helping small businesses through programs, loans, enterprise zones, and assistance. Check to see whether your community has a similar agency. These agencies and programs can be a great source of information and capital.

In addition, state and federal governments might offer tax benefits if you hire minorities, disabled workers, or teens during the summer. Check around. The Minority Business Development Agency (http://www.mbda.gov) was created to help minority businesses grow. It has nine regional centers.

Anyone can benefit from locating a business in an urban enterprise zone (UEZ) or a "brownfield." A brownfield is a tract of land that has been developed for industrial purposes and abandoned and is usually located in disadvantaged parts of cities or blighted former industrial sites. Companies that set up shop in brownfields are offered tax incentives and government aid.

Also, minorities and women can benefit from grants issued by foundations and the government. Some grants come from specific groups as awards for entrepreneurship. Others come from groups dedicated to helping those in similar circumstances. Sometimes your local government can give you further information. Chapter 13 has resources as well.

Private Investors

Angel Investors
Typically, many companies start out with an investment from a wealthy individual or a group of wealthy individuals known as angel investors. They provide modest capital for a start-up usually in exchange for convertible debt or ownership equity in the company. Steve Jobs and Steve Wozniak got their first funding for the Apple II computer from Mike Markkula, an early investor in the company.

Angels can be friends and family, but that doesn't mean that complete informality is appropriate. Have your attorney write up appropriate paperwork for these investors so they get their proper return on their investment. Angel groups come from everywhere—communities, university alumni groups, and local businesspeople who pool their money to grow more jobs in their communities.

Most angel investments can go from a few thousand dollars up to $3 million. *Inc.* magazine publishes a leading independent directory of angel investors. Start your reading there.

Venture Capitalists

Venture capitalists are the next rung of private investment, and they tend to service small businesses with promising growth that have been around for a year or more. Venture capitalists tend to operate more formally, actually establishing common pools of money that they might invest in a portfolio of companies at once.

Venture capitalists are not parents, cousins, or high school buddies. They operate more like professional investment managers who deal only with professional prospects.

There are many books that can help you better understand the venture capital process better than this one, but the shorthand on attracting venture capital goes something like this:

- Establish a track record in a unique business idea.
- Shape your company into a solid business operation.
- Start looking for the venture capital network that makes sense for you (Techcrunch.com is a good starting place).
- Start learning the language of venture capitalists and learn to present yourself and your company to them.

Few start-ups will be financed this way, so the best route is to start your business, grow, and then prepare a proposal for an appropriate firm.

Put it this way: if you're attracting venture capital money to your business, you're doing pretty well.

QUICK Tip

Get Creative: You may be privy to other sources of capital, such as inheritance, stock, garage sale revenue, or rainy-day money stuffed into a mason jar. We're getting pretty far fetched here for a reason. We want you to search for capital in any and every avenue or venue possible. Do not overlook any potential legal source of capital.

Stock

When people talk about a business issuing stock, they're usually talking about an initial public offering, or IPO. Small businesses tend to be focused on more intermediate forms of stock ownership to make sure initial investors get paid. That's what we're going to be talking about here.

Selling stock can bring capital to your company in the form of shareholder's equity. Stock is an issuance of ownership in a company. It is usually affected by a sale of a certificate for money to an individual or organization. When you start a corporation, you will have a certain number of shares issued at start-up. This might be all the capital you need.

In early 2012, President Obama signed the Jumpstart Our Business Start-ups (JOBS) Act, which provided several key advantages for small companies to raise funds. It provided two key provisions for smaller companies:

1. Allowing small businesses to harness "crowdfunding." Building on early models like Kickstarter.com, once the U.S. Securities and Exchange Commission (SEC) sets specific rules, start-ups and small businesses will be allowed to raise up to $1 million annually from many small-dollar investors through web-based platforms, thus democratizing access to capital.
2. Expanding "mini public offerings." The bill has made it easier to file IPOs of less than $50 million in market capitalization.

There are other options for stock issuance for small companies. Direct public offerings (DPOs) allow a company to raise capital by marketing its shares directly to its own customers, employees, suppliers, distributors, and friends in the community. The paperwork needs to be overseen by an attorney with experience in these areas, but this is not a process with the typical expense and procedures of an actual IPO.

Getting Creative

Get a Part-Time or Seasonal Job
A part-time job before, during, or after your start-up can provide capital and will be proof to potential investors and lenders that you are serious about financing your business. Although you will not raise a lot of money this way, it is a viable option, especially if you are starting a SOHO or microbusiness.

Reporting Your Progress: If you receive a bank loan or capital from other people, you must keep the bank or investors informed of your company's progress. A banker should see monthly financials, including your cash-flow statements, balance sheets, and receivables. Also, explain the things the loan is doing for your company in terms of inventory, marketing, personnel, capital purchases, and/or sales. The financials are more important, though. Your banker is, in essence, a partner who has a vested interest in your company. It is worth your while to work with him or her before, during, and after getting a loan.

Use Another Business's Assets

Maybe you have one part-time business with cash flow but limited growth opportunities. This business could provide eventual start-up capital for a future business with much more growth potential. For example, you may have a well-known blog that provides income through advertising, but has no further possibilities for expansion. Using the capital provided through your blog, you may be able to fund an entrepreneurial project or write a book that may bring in more opportunities for income and growth.

Barter for What You Need

Business barter exchanges are a relatively new, but expanding, phenomenon. Here you will exchange your goods or services for other goods and services with participating companies. You might sell your product for free accounting from an accountant or for auto work on your company vehicle from a garage. Many local exchanges have been set up. If your city has one, simply call up or drop by for some information.

The tax implications of a barter exchange are something to consider, as is the fact that you do not get capital in the traditional sense. It is more like working capital in the form of goods or services received—or virtual capital. Still, this can get you services and products that otherwise you'd have to part with capital to receive. It might cut into your profitability, but it will enable you to run your business with less start-up money.

Sell Some of Your Assets

Some people sell lake cottages, homes, cars, furniture, stamp or coin collections, and other possessions to start their businesses. You will have to be careful because you don't want to sell something you'll want or need later on. The key here is to sell what you can, like a vacation home or a third car that no one in the family is using.

If you have stock options at your current job or mutual funds, you can sell these to fund your new venture. It probably isn't prudent to dip into any individual retirement accounts for this purpose, though. Get advice from your accountant and attorney. If you own another business, you might consider selling it to finance your new start-up.

If you are unable to raise capital, you might have to revise your business plan or put your venture on hold. Again, the best way to get money is to make some first. That is why most businesses must start small. Don't give up, though. Some companies have started small and have grown very large, but some have started big and failed. In essence, capital is very important, but it must be used properly in conjunction with your plan and your goals.

Stockholder Meetings: Send your stock investors annual reports at the end of the fiscal year. We suggest that you provide quarterly or monthly updates as well, explaining what the company did the past month or months. Investors will appreciate these updates. In addition, you are required to hold stockholder's meetings, which you should do on an annual basis. You will invite your investors to the meeting and discuss the company's progress thus far, vote on issues, and get a chance to talk face-to-face with your backers. Hold it on a weekend so everyone can come.

Chapter 9

Getting Social

If there's a line that most small business people hear, it's that you have to wear many hats in your own company. Among them are chief executive officer; receptionist; salesperson; bookkeeper; janitor; stocker; hiring officer; complaint department; and, most certainly, prognosticator, for your ability to see the future.

Today, more than ever, seeing the future means taking more aspects of your business online. Most companies, large and small, have done that already in the form of traditional websites and email connectivity. But it's time for the next wave—social media and wherever it leads.

Being in business today means being a communicator. That may not be your primary skill, but don't panic, because you can always find help to do that. However, many of you may already know something about social media. You may already be active users of Facebook, Twitter, LinkedIn, and beyond. And if you're not, maybe your kids and younger friends and colleagues are.

In any event, you need to investigate how social media can help your business. It may help a little, or a lot.

What Is Social Media?

Everyone is talking about social media, but let's define it first. Social media starts with the Internet. That's your highway to websites that allow people to talk to one another in different ways—through text (similar to sending email messages); through audio and visuals (taking a digital photo, video, music file, graphic, or other set of static or moving digital material that can be uploaded online); or through links that take a potential recipient to news stories, personal writings, or virtually any document that exists.

So what's social media? Anything you see online that allows you to talk, share, or show. And yes, when people talk about social media in the world of business, they're likely to mention brand names like Facebook, Twitter, and LinkedIn. Those are the leaders as this book was published. Will they be the leading brands a year after you read these words? Tough to say. Is anyone still using Friendster or MySpace? Case in point.

Like everything else on the Internet, things change, and better mousetraps can take hold in a period of days, weeks, or months.

QUICK Tip

Tracking Trends: How can you keep track of social media trends and overall technology issues? Where's the best place to learn about what's going on online? Well, online, of course. As of mid-2012, these were some of the top sites. To find who's new on this ever-changing list, do a search for "top technology sites" and see who pops up:

- **AllThingsDigital (http://allthingsd.com):** The *Wall Street Journal's* big overview site on technology issues big and small.
- **Bits (http://bits.blogs.nytimes.com):** A daily sift of the best product and trend news from the *New York Times'* tech reporters.
- **Mashable (http://mashable.com):** A leading independent site with a special focus on social media among all major tech topics.
- **GigaOm (http://gigaom.com):** Great overall site talking about Internet-based trends in business that are relevant particularly to small companies.
- **Inc.com (http://www.inc.com/managing-technology):** The tech channel of the leading small business website *Inc.* magazine.
- **Entrepreneur.com (http://www.entrepreneur.com/tech nology/index.html):** Turn to this longtime start-up business magazine's tech channel for the latest on all business issues moving online.

Why Is Social Media Important to a Business?

What if you had a chance to reach potential customers or clients any time of the day or night to tell them what was new with your business, what was on sale, or what they might want to buy in the future from you? That's just one of the things social media can help you accomplish. It's an outbound conversation that never quits.

But there's an inbound factor, too. In putting your identity out there, you're collecting people who hopefully have a natural interest in what you're selling (the terms *followers* and *friends* are most commonly used), so social media is something like an ever-developing marketing list and a broadcast channel all at once.

Is the Traditional Website Dead?

No, the traditional website is not dead. But it's changing.

For some people, their traditional website is more of a blog (an online journal that can be updated at will) or their Facebook or LinkedIn page.

Put it this way. Your business is always going to need a home on the Internet that's completely within your control, a place where you define what your company is and does. Consider it a hub or mother ship to support all the ways you reach out to potential customers or for them to reach you.

Many people reach out to web designers and writers to create these centralized online presences for them, and if that's not your central expertise, that's fine—it's good to bring in help, if only as a sounding board. But the process is getting to be much more do-it-yourself.

For instance, the once-static web page that you'd update just to change an address or phone number has evolved into formats that allow the owner—you—to change content much more easily at will and to hold a regular conversation with your audience.

Yes, we're talking about blogging, a term that's also in a constant state of evolution. Early on, *blogging* was a term for online journaling. Today, it's evolved into the dominant form of web presence because it allows owners to display the static features they need to (what the business is, where it is, and how it can be reached) with a dynamic element that allows owners to talk to their audience on a constant basis.

But instead of telling, let's show.

Making a Choice

Even for those who live and work in the technology industry, making a choice on the best blogging software, the best social media choices, and the best marketing strategy is dizzying because there's something new every day. Here's how to deal with that woozy feeling:

1. **Jump in.** Start trying out social media as an individual. Find out what's good and bad about it, then apply what you're learning to your own business model.

2. **Network.** Either online or in person, start reaching out to people who are talking about these topics and seem to know what they're doing.

3. **Ask lots of questions.** Yes, people will tell you some of your questions are stupid. Keep asking anyway.

4. **Always ask if there's a cheaper solution.** Experts can help you customize an idea or message. But in small business, you need to always ask if there's a do-it-yourself or crowdsourced solution (*crowdsourcing* means getting others involved online to help you) that might keep costs and workload down.

QUICK Tip

The Blog as Website, and Vice Versa: If you want to get a sense of how modern companies—small and large—are telling their stories online, go visit the leading purveyors of blogging software. Sometimes free, sometimes for a fee, these major outlets are a great way to get ideas about your own presence online, and yes, you can either create your own site or get a professional involved:

- **Wordpress (http://www.wordpress.org):** You'll hear the phrases "blogging tool" and "content management system" applied to this site, and you can spend all day learning what those things are in other books and elsewhere on the web. Here's what's important. This, at the moment of publication, is the number-one resource for most people building modern websites with a blogging feature. Stop by, wander around, and see what's getting built.
- **Tumblr (http://www.tumblr.com):** Like Wordpress, Tumblr is a software site. Experts call this a "microblogging" site because it's not heavy in bells and whistles like menus and links and a lot of other features common to traditional websites. But many would argue that for some people, Tumblr sites work fine as websites because they allow for little verbiage and lots of images on a daily basis with basic contact information. Check the examples at the site. One might be right for you.
- **Blogger (http://www.blogger.com):** The first, and for many, still the best. A couple of keystrokes, and you're online. Sort of the midpoint between a Tumblr and a Wordpress these days—customizable, but not too customizable, and there's usually a template that fits everyone's needs.

Are there more? Certainly. Do a search on "top blogging software," see what pops up, and start checking examples.

5. **Set aside time every day to learn.** Try to keep it the same time every day with a fixed start and stop. You might spend the day surfing otherwise.

Be Smart about Technology Spending

Technology is a part of every business these days, whether it involves computer-driven production equipment in a factory or office environment or a low-cost laptop needed to keep your business and personal finances in order.

Here are two rules to follow:

1. Scale your technology spending with what the business actually needs at the time.
2. Get smart advice to control overall capital equipment spending.

Keep Investment Low

In the fatter economic times that ended definitively in 2007, it was easy for fledgling businesses to be talked into "new" technology investment, because everyone believed double-digit economic growth would support it. Five years later, the United States and most of the world was wrestling with the aftermath of the toughest economic slowdown in seventy years.

Spending habits have changed throughout the business world. As a new businessperson, it might be wise to adopt the conservative 2012 spending habits and keep them throughout the life of your business.

Every business has particular technology it needs to invest in. Here are some critical questions to ask before you spend:

- What is the minimal technology everyone in my business will need to do their jobs effectively?
- Can that technology be new or used?
- Are there shared solutions we can take advantage of, such as cloud computing solutions (free or for a fee) available on the Internet?
- Is my capital investment plan based on buying in emergencies, or is there a real plan for investment over time in cutting-edge hardware and software as we're scaling the business?
- Can we pay cash?

It's a new ball game—financing for small business has always been tight, and as the latest edition of this book was being planned, conditions were among the tightest in many decades. Realistically, some start-ups will have to take advantage of credit to buy what they need. But the smartest business owners will focus their cash and credit resources on people first, since they'll be the first outreach to the customer, and to the best technological resources after that.

QUICK Tip

The Cloud: For smart technology that's free, go to the cloud. Small business people should always look for smart, low-cost business solutions first. Internet-based software solutions—better known as "cloud computing"—are a good first stop. Here are some ideas you might want to consider:

- **Document and project software:** Google Docs is giving market leader Microsoft Word a run for its money because it costs you nothing and allows you to collaborate on projects no matter where your partners are in the world. Plus, it allows you to save that work on your hard drive in a variety of formats, including Word.
- **Financial software:** While small business accounting software has been around for more than a decade, free solutions are a good way to give a fledgling company cash, spending, saving, and investing capabilities until it needs to spend for more sophisticated software and solutions. Mint.com provides a great basic money management tool that can help small business owners start out until they need more functionality.
- **Image editing:** Whether you're a professional writing business or a business that needs to manage its own communications, there are free tools online that will help you edit still images as well as video. YouTube.com has a variety of cloud-based editing tools at http://www.youtube.com/create.

There are plenty more free tools out there. Go search!

Bring Your Advisers into the Loop

Think all lawyers and accountants are good for is legal and tax stuff? Make them work a few muscles, and ask them what they would recommend for your overall capital investments as well as their timing. Keep in mind that these are experts who deal with many kinds of businesses and business owners, and they have valuable perspective outside the immediate needs of your business. So come armed with questions anytime you talk to them.

Chapter 10

Taxes and Insurance

- ◗ Social Security taxes
- ◗ Federal unemployment tax
- ◗ Income withholding
- ◗ Business income taxes
- ◗ Sales and use taxes
- ◗ Property taxes
- ◗ Inventory taxes
- ◗ Business insurance
- ◗ Personal insurance

As they say, two things are certain in life—death and taxes. If a third certainty were to be added to that phrase, it would be insurance.

You need to understand these three inevitabilities before you get into business because, depending on the kind of business you run, the impact might be enough to convince you not to try the business.

The financial implications of taxes and insurance are some of the particular reasons anyone starting a company needs to confer with qualified legal, accounting, and personal finance help first.

Taxes and insurance can both heap burdensome costs on your small business. Taxes are unavoidable. Insurance is trickier. You may or may not need certain types of insurance for your business and employees. This is where an accountant and an insurance agent come in handy to explain the particulars of taxes and insurance and the associated costs of each.

Taxes

As we discussed in chapter 6, taxes are a consideration when deciding the type of business entity you will form. Again, this is why you should consult a tax expert who understands the landscape in your home state as well as other states in which you plan to operate.

QUICK Tip

Online Sales Tax: If you are a retail business planning to sell online, your tax issues may not be national now, but they might be someday. While so-called nexus laws requiring retailers to collect sales taxes where customers live have affected primarily larger companies, small businesses need to stay vigilant on the tax front, particularly since so many states are running at a deficit.

Every working adult has paid taxes before, but probably not to the extent you will when you run a small business. And paying them yourself makes you understand more fully the consequences of taxes on your bottom line. The basic taxes are shown in figure 10.1.

In fact, many business owners cite regulations and taxes as among the biggest hindrances to business because they pull money and resources from companies. Although we could argue the fairness of taxing very small businesses at all (we feel that there should be a minimum floor to reach before your small business is taxed), the fact is that taxes are for the good of society and we have to deal with them.

Again, your entity choice may have the greatest effect on the final amount of taxes you pay, and that's why it's important to evaluate your tax circumstances continually throughout the life of your business. As we mentioned, if you incorporate your business, you'll be facing a tax hit at the corporate level and again at the personal level; sole proprietorships, limited liability companies, and S corporations have only single taxation. The complexity of a business adds complexity to the tax picture as well.

Small businesses with employees have additional taxation issues to consider. Your payroll system will have to withdraw a variety of local, state, and national taxes and keep track of benefits you offer as well. Also keep in mind that, as the employer, you will be paying a share of each employee's Social Security tax.

QUICK Tip

Think Taxes Are a Pain? Keep in mind that certain regulated businesses have fees and extra taxation to contend with, including special business licenses for states and municipalities. Again, this should be part of your due diligence before you make the final decision to start your business.

State and local governments may charge a range of taxes on sales, income, and property, but they might levy fees for utilities, sanitation, and other shared services government provides. So now you need to consider whether owning versus renting provides a win-lose to the business and whether your business can cover the cost of the government-provided services you're going to be using.

Larger firms incur more tax burdens than simple SOHO businesses that operate out of the proprietor's home.

Taxes affect your start-up because they will eat into your capital and will remain a constant cost of business. A complicated tax situation generally makes an accountant and a business attorney a must, so consult chapter 14 for resources in your state. Experienced experts in these areas not only help you save money on taxes but also might be able to help you get tax relief through federal minority programs, certain employment programs, local economic development initiatives, and urban enterprise zones if you qualify.

Social Security Taxes

Anyone who employs people is responsible for Federal Insurance Contribution taxes, better known as FICA, or Social Security tax. You even owe for yourself if you are self-employed (simply called the "self-employment tax"). The current tax rate is 7.65 percent for employees, and the employer pays 7.65 percent. As your own employee, you will pay a 15.3 percent self-employed tax. Unless you meet certain requirements, you'll pay estimated taxes on a quarterly basis.

There are two parts to FICA: Old Age, Survivors, and Disability Insurance (OASDI) and Hospital Insurance (HI), often just called Medicare. The 2012 OASDI is 6.2 percent on maximum taxable earnings of $110,100 (6.2 percent for employers and 4.20 percent for employees, and HI is 1.45 percent for employers and employees).

Figure 10.1: FORMS OF TAXATION

There are several basic types of taxes your business might incur. Study the rest of this chapter for a more in-depth discussion of each form of taxation.

Federal taxes include the following:

- **Social Security taxes**
- **Federal unemployment taxes**
- **Income withholding**
- **Business income taxes**

State taxes include the following:

- **Income withholding**
- **Sales and use taxes**

- **Business income taxes**

Local taxes usually include the following:

- **Property taxes**
- **Excise or use taxes on certain goods and services**
- **City or county economic development or income taxes**

Federal Unemployment Tax

The Federal Unemployment Tax Act provides for a quarterly tax for compensation to workers who have lost their jobs. It is collected and then used in unemployment payments after an employee has been laid off. The 2012 rate is 6 percent and applies to the first $7,000 in wages you pay per year. After that, you have no further burden.

In addition, your state may require you to file a report with it listing your tax liability. Contact your state for information on unemployment tax.

Income Withholding

As employees, withholding is something we are all familiar with. If you employ people or pay yourself, you will be responsible for using government formulas to determine income withholding amounts on each paycheck. Partners, sole proprietors, limited liability company members, and shareholders may be required to pay quarterly estimated taxes to the government on Form 1040-ES. Other businesses such as corporations with many employees will pay quarterly withholding taxes on federal Form 941.

The 2012 personal tax rates are as follows:

Bracket	Married, Filing Jointly	Single
10%	$0–$17,400	$0–$8,700
15%	$17,400–$70,700	$8,700–$35,350
25%	$70,700–$142,700	$35,350–$85,650
28%	$142,700–$217,450	$85,650–$178,650
33%	$217,450–$388,350	$178,650–$388,350
35%	Over $388,350	Over $388,350

State and local income withholding taxes vary (see appendix B). As small business owners, you will generally pay the same way as you do for federal taxes—quarterly, with a "coupon" that you send to the state revenue department. Check your state revenue office for further information—you'll find that contact information in chapter 14.

Business Income Taxes

Corporations are the only entity taxed twice, once at the corporate level and once at the stockholder's level. All other major business entities are taxed once. Income reporting methods vary for different business entities:

- Sole proprietors report income on their Form 1040 and on Schedule C or C-EZ.
- Partnerships report on the Form 1040 and on Form 1065.
- Limited liability companies report their business income on their regular income tax form and on Form 1065.
- C corporations will report income on Form 1120 or 1120A.
- S corporations report income on Form 1120S.

In 2012, federal corporate tax rates ranged from 15 percent to 39.2 percent. Appendix B has a complete list of corporate state tax rates.

Most states have income taxes for corporations, and some might for other entities such as partnerships and limited liability companies. These laws change constantly, so the best bet here is to contact your state for its requirements. You might want to call your state's Small Business Development Center for information as well.

Sales and Use Taxes

As consumers, we understand the concept of paying sales taxes well enough, but as a business owner, you will need to collect sales tax depending on your state requirements (see appendix B). Some states have no sales tax. Use taxes, which are levied on purchases bought out of state to escape sales and other local taxes, may be a further burden.

Most states will require you to pay these use taxes in a similar manner to your sales taxes. Some states will also levy excise taxes on such things as sales of gasoline, liquor, and tobacco.

Sales taxes can be exempt on purchases you make with the intent of reselling the goods. The tax will be due when you sell the goods to the consumer. If you resell what you purchase, you will receive a sales tax exemption. You file for this number when you register your business with your revenue department. Most forms have check-off boxes allowing you to apply for a variety of taxes and for exemption. After you get the exemption, most states will have you fill out exempt forms every time you purchase goods this way. You give this form to the seller and pay no sales tax until you resell the goods.

Excise taxes are other forms of state taxes and will affect certain businesses, including wholesalers and retailers. Your state or Small Business Development Center can provide more information.

QUICK Tip

Tax Payment: Most small businesses will pay monthly or quarterly estimated or actual sales tax, depending on sales volume and amount owed. The state will likely give you a "coupon" booklet or sheet with statements for you to fill out and submit with your check. More and more states are moving to electronic funds transfer to accomplish this.

Property Taxes

If you own your office or factory, you will naturally owe property taxes on your land and your plant or office. These vary from state to state. Most property taxes are paid to your county or township assessor's office either yearly or twice a year. Some are paid through mortgages.

Inventory Taxes

Inventory taxes are due on your inventory of goods in, say, a warehouse or factory at a specific time of the year. You create an inventory for your goods and then submit a form and a check to the state. The idea is to tax the goods you have yet to sell (or have not been able to sell). Some states are doing away with these taxes, and we hope all will eventually.

During the 1990s, some states did away with inventory taxes and some sales taxes, lowered other sales tax rates, and lowered vehicle excise taxes and property taxes as a result of other sources of revenue (notably gaming and lottery proceeds). Still, the effect of taxation is great, and because of lower federal funding of certain state-managed programs at the start of the millennium, some states have had to look into raising taxes again.

To pay taxes, use the coupon booklets the federal government or your state sends you; also, many states give you the option to pay online through automated balance debiting. Regardless of the method, you are still responsible for paying taxes. Talk to your accountant about this.

Most companies, except sole proprietorships, will file for a federal Employer Identification Number (EIN, on IRS Form SS-4), which registers you with the IRS. Take your federal ID number with you to register for state sales, excise, and withholding taxes. If you do not have it when you register, you may be able to send it to the state revenue office later. Check your state's requirements to see if the EIN is even needed for state registration if you are a sole proprietor.

If you sell a product, you must record sales tax for the state in which the product is sold. If you sell via mail, you will collect tax only from residents of the state in which your business exists. Again, to purchase merchandise for resale, you will need a state sales tax exemption number. In some states, your sales tax number allows you to buy merchandise without paying sales tax. Once you resell it, you can collect the tax. In some states, when you collect sales tax, you keep a percentage because you are acting as the collection agent for that tax. This is not true in all cases, but it is in many. Consult your state for its requirements.

Remember, most taxes (Social Security, withholding) must be paid quarterly if the total is $1,000 or more. In addition, Form 941 is filed for quarterly returns. Form 940 EZ or 940 will be sent for year-end FUTA tax returns, which are typically due January 31. The W2s are due to the employee at the end of January, and the federal copy is due at the IRS on February 28.

The states generally send simple forms and envelopes for withholding taxes and sales tax, although recently some have switched to an electronic transfer system for withholding over a certain amount. This money is automatically transferred from your bank to the state. Your state may have a similar program.

Business tax returns, such as for income, are due within four months after the company's tax year ends. This is important to remember. If you do not get them by mid-January, write for them, or better yet, go to your accountant. Also make sure you get your hands on Publication 15 (Circular E), better known as the *Employer's Tax Guide*, which is a guide on business returns at the federal level.

QUICK Tip

The IRS Online: The IRS website makes it possible to download any tax form, and the IRS now has a very useful center for all forms specifically relevant to small business. Go to http://www.irs.gov and type "Small Business and Self-Employed Tax Center" in the search box. The center offers virtually everything a new business owner needs, including up-to-date publications on the federal tax system that also include notes on local, county, and state tax systems.

Understanding taxes is one of the cornerstones of business success. Being unfamiliar with new tax laws and the numerous deductions, allowances, and so on, can cost you thousands of dollars over the years and many lost work hours. To take advantage of great money-saving deductions and allowances, we suggest hiring a competent tax accountant, reading books about taxes, studying deductions and allowances, and utilizing the existing IRS services.

Proper tax planning includes setting up the right business entity, taking advantage of deductions, setting realistic goals, maintaining cash flow, and keeping expenses low. By making it a habit to read newspaper, magazine, and journal articles on taxes, you and your company stand a better chance of being informed of tax changes that may affect your business.

Changes in tax laws occur annually. Numerous books and software programs exist for tax preparation and information, some of which you will find listed in chapter 13.

The SBA and IRS offer ways for entrepreneurs to brush up on their tax knowledge. The SBA often holds seminars and the IRS sponsors the Volunteer Income Tax Assistance program. This program gives you the opportunity to keep current on tax regulations while helping others with their tax returns. The IRS instructors teach you how to prepare such forms as the 1040EZ, 1040A, and the basic 1040 at no cost to you. This is a great educational program.

Other IRS programs, often held at local offices, are geared toward specific business tax issues and are held throughout the year. A good place to check is the IRS website or your local IRS office.

Finally, most state departments of revenue hold tax seminars for new and growing businesses. Issues include payroll taxes, sales taxes, excise taxes, and franchise taxes, to name a few. These are low- or no-cost ways of educating yourself or your staff (if applicable) and keeping abreast of state tax laws and filing methods. These are often run by the SBA, Small Business Development Centers, or revenue field offices. See chapter 13 for more information, and connect with your state revenue office.

Insurance

Depending on the kind of business you're operating, you need to have a discussion with a trusted insurance agent about benefits and liability coverage for yourself and your employees, as well as liability coverage for the business itself.

It's important to realize that legal protections afforded through your business entity may not be enough.

QUICK Tip

Insurance Experts: Insurance professionals should be included on your team of business experts. Finding a good insurance agent may be as simple as getting referrals from friends or business associates or through your tax and financial advisers. In any event, it's critical to sit down and discuss all potential insurance needs and risks to make sure you're protecting your personal and business assets and your livelihood.

For the new small office and home office company, insurance needs may be minimal. You may need insurance just for yourself or for inventory. However, larger small businesses may need a wide range of insurance covering inventory, liability, theft, employee health and life plans, and workers' compensation insurance. Many companies with full-time employees provide some form of health insurance and sick-time benefits. Often, this is a combination of employee and employer contributions on the insurance side.

Ask your advisers to outline what they think your needs will be and anything you should do to make pricing more affordable. At the very least, one main consideration before start-up is making sure that you have health and disability coverage before you leave your existing employer. Disability coverage is based in part on insuring the majority of earnings you're making now, and once you start your business, you may not be getting an actual paycheck for a while.

Figure 10.2: **EXPERT ACCOUNTING ADVICE**

An accountant will help you take advantage of the following full or partial tax deductions:

- Lawyer's fees against liability claims
- Accounting expenses for audits, bookkeeping, and tax-return preparation
- Business taxes, except federal income taxes, which are deductible
- Cars used in the business (or your car if it is used for business)
- Bank account charges (for checking account)
- Charitable contributions
- Depreciation
- Repairs
- Insurance premiums
- Interest on business loans
- Business loses and bad debts
- Office rent
- Maintenance
- Salaries
- Merchandise costs
- Travel expenses when conducted for business
- Uniforms
- Social Security taxes you pay for employees
- Office expenses and supplies
- Salaries
- Dues to business organizations
- Small business owner health insurance premiums

The key with insurance is to be covered no matter what. No one likes making insurance payments, but there comes a time when you will be glad you did.

Chapter

11

Regulations and Licenses

▶ **Fair wages**

▶ **Equal opportunity and civil rights**

▶ **Worker safety**

▶ **Labor relations**

▶ **Fair treatment**

▶ **Benefits**

The previous chapter outlined the particular tax burden on small business. Regulations (and to a smaller extent, licensing requirements) are also part and parcel of external government influences and restrictions on small business.

Legislators and regulators have influence over how we employ workers, produce and sell goods, and develop companies. Most regulations were enacted to redress a real or perceived wrong, threat, or inequality. Over the years, a steady stream of government regulations has been enacted so that business owners now face hundreds of local, state, and federal regulations that affect all or particular industries. See figure 11.1 for an indication of the impact of regulatory costs on small businesses.

Figure 11.1 Distribution of Regulatory Compliance Costs by Firm Size in 2008

Type of Regulation	Cost per Employee			
	All Firms	Firms with <20 Employees	Firms with 20–499 Employees	Firms with 500+ Employees
All Federal Regulations	$8,086	$10,585	$7,454	$7,755
Economic	$5,153	$4,120	$4,750	$5,835
Environmental	$1,523	$4,101	$1,294	$883
Tax Compliance	$800	$1,584	$760	$517
Occupational Safety and Health, and Homeland Security	$610	$781	$650	$520

*Notes to Figure 11.1

Milton Friedman put the estimated burden of government mandates and regulations at roughly 10 percent of U.S. national income in 2003. See Milton Friedman, "What Every American Wants," *Wall Street Journal,* January 15, 2003, p. A10.

Source: "The Impact of Regulatory Costs on Small Firms," Nicole V. Crain and W. Mark Crain, Lafayette College, Easton, PA, September 2010, SBA Office of Advocacy.

Despite the overwhelming amount of regulations, they have in essence become a part of doing business like paying taxes and giving out sales receipts. Regulations must be dealt with as a hindrance but not a blockage to doing business. If your company grows, sooner or later most simple regulations will cease to have a negative effect on the company. But that's when other regulations start affecting your business, and especially your employment and benefits practices. No one business can get around all regulations, but not all regulations apply to any one business. The key is to not panic but to deal with regulations in constructive ways.

Small business regulations are created and enforced by local, state, and federal governments and typically affect the following areas: employment pay and working conditions, property use and zoning, pollution, product sales and service, advertising, warranties, and communications. Most industries have industry-specific regulations to adhere to, many of which are environmental in nature. Other regulations, like minimum wages, affect almost all employers, large and small. Add regulatory responsibilities to the list of topics that you and your attorney should discuss in planning your business.

Local and state regulations are somewhat easier to deal with because your chance at redress is greater than federal regulations. See figure 11.2 for a quick run down of some of the regulations that should be familiar to you.

QUICK Tip

Mind Those Regulations: Many small business owners face local zoning laws, registration rules, and wage guidelines. Understanding these basics is your first area of regulatory study before you start your business. It might be wise to start a notebook or computer file for initial paperwork related to these rules and to keep steady records on compliance in case questions come up.

City and county zoning laws were created to monitor residential, commercial, and industrial sites in specific areas of communities. When you start your business, you must adhere to these laws, even if you operate a home office where there is little or no business traffic. If you need to use your home outside that purpose, it is best to investigate the rules and apply for a zoning variance if necessary.

Corporations tend to face the widest array of regulations because of their stock ownership model—among other things, they have to register the names of board members and managers and make quarterly reports on operations. As organizations grow, they typically add further rules and regulations to their responsibilities.

Yet the smallest of companies have their respective requirements. It's important to plan for minimum wage levels and mandated local, state, and federal withholding in your workforce planning, assuming that you're hiring employees.

Since size plays a big part in determining the number of regulations affecting a business, many federal regulations, like the Family and Medical Leave Act of 1993, tend to exempt businesses of fewer than fifty employees. However, you should keep these and other regulations in mind as you plan future growth. You may choose to adhere to certain nonbinding regulations because of size; it might make good business sense to do so out of principle or for ethical reasons. This puts you in a good light with employees, the community, and customers.

Immigration and foreign worker regulatory compliance has become a much bigger employee responsibility since the September 11, 2001, terrorist attacks. You must complete U.S. Citizenship and Immigration Services Form I-9 Employment Eligibility Verification for each employee. The U.S. Citizenship and Immigration Services website (http://www.uscis.gov) has that form and others available for download so you can have the proper DHS paperwork. Since September 11, the federal government has demanded stricter reporting of noncitizen workers, so make sure you adhere to these regulations.

Along with regulations come licensing requirements. If you incorporate in any of the regulated professions, seek legal, governmental, and published sources of information before you incorporate. These professions include accountants, bankers, insurance, doctors and dentists, engineers, hotels, lawyers, real estate agents, liquor stores, teachers, detectives, and restaurants, just to name a tiny fraction.

If you are such a professional, you probably already know your certification and licensing requirements. But be aware that you need to confirm the status of those you hire.

QUICK Tip

Check on Licensing: Licensing occurs at the state level and is usually handled by a state agency. Sometimes licenses are required at the city level, so check with the city clerk.

Figure 11.2: IMPORTANT SMALL BUSINESS REGULATIONS TO CONSIDER

Local, state, and federal regulations must all be taken into account whenever you plan a business. The more you understand and work with the regulations, the better your chances for success.

- **Federal Trade Commission Act (unfair trade)**
- **Fair Packaging and Labeling Act**
- **Mansion-Moss Warranty Act (warranties)**
- **UCC—the Uniform Commercial Code (sales contracts)**
- **Truth in Lending Act (disclosure of credit terms)**
- **Fair Credit Reporting Act (protection of personal credit)**

In addition, as a prospective employer, you must be aware of federal, state, and local laws regarding workplace conduct. They begin with rules about questions you can and cannot ask during job interviews and go from there. You do not want to get burned by accidentally breaking the law in your first time as a business owner.

Some regulations are voluntary, but you might want to consider following them on ethical, goodwill, or networking grounds. The Better Business Bureau, chambers of commerce, and industry groups recommend best practices in a host of areas to help businesses observe high ethical and operating standards. Many groups require potential members to sign off on these standards before they will be accredited or approved as members.

The following is a general listing of regulations that most employers experience no matter what the size of their company. Your attorney; accountant; and state commerce, labor, and revenue offices (see chapter 14) can give you a more specific idea of what you need to know to operate locally.

Fair Wages

- **The Fair Labor Standards Act (FLSA).** Sets standards for wages and overtime pay in the private and public sector. For specifics, go to the website of the Wage and Hour Division at the U.S. Department of Labor website (http://www.dol.gov). As of 2012, the federal minimum wage was $7.25 an hour.
- **Contract Work Hours and Safety Standards Act of 1962.** Covers hours and safety standards in construction contracts.
- **Equal Pay Act of 1963.** Prohibits discrimination in pay based on sex.
- **Walsh-Healy Act.** Sets minimum wages for federal contractors of $10,000 or more and prohibits the employment of youths younger than age sixteen and convicts except under certain conditions.
- **Davis-Bacon Act.** Minimum wage for federally funded public works projects in excess of $2,000.

Equal Opportunity and Civil Rights

- **Civil Rights Act of 1964.** Makes it unlawful for employers with fifteen or more employees to discriminate against people on the basis of race, color, religion, national origin, or sex in regards to hiring and employment.
- **Age Discrimination in Employment Act of 1967.** Prohibits firms with twenty or more employees from discriminating against workers forty years old or older.
- **Equal Employment Opportunity Act of 1972.** Prohibits firms with twenty or more employees from discriminating against workers on the basis of race, color, sex, national origin, or religion.
- **Rehabilitation Act of 1973.** Prohibits discrimination against physically or mentally handicapped persons in federal contracts.
- **Pregnancy Discrimination Act of 1978.** Requires that employers treat pregnancy just as they do other medical issues.
- **Immigration Reform and Control Act of 1986.** Employers must verify employees' proof of citizenship and legal residency in the United States. Each employer must keep a completed federal Form I-9 for each employee hired after 1986. This is an important business requirement.
- **Americans with Disabilities Act of 1990.** Prohibits employers with fifteen or more employees from discriminating against handicapped persons and requires them to provide accommodations that do not pose an undue hardship.

- **Older Workers Benefit Protection Act of 1990.** Prohibits discrimination with respect to employee benefits on the basis of age and regulates early retirement benefits.
- **Lilly Ledbetter Fair Pay Act of 2009.** Amends the Civil Rights Act of 1964 stating that the 180-day statute of limitations for filing an equal-pay lawsuit regarding pay discrimination resets with each new discriminatory paycheck.

Worker Safety

- **Occupational Safety and Health Act of 1970 (OSHA).** Employers must provide safe working conditions for workers. An addition to OSHA is the Hazard Communication Standard, which is a system of informing employees about hazards and how to respond to them.

Labor Relations

- **National Labor Relations Act of 1935 (Wagner Act).** Gives employees the right to unionize.
- **Taft-Hartley Act of 1947.** Addresses rights of employers and unions in regard to job actions, negotiations, and organizing.
- **Landrum-Griffin Act of 1957.** Gives rights to members within the union.

Fair Treatment

- **Employee Polygraph Protection Act of 1988.** Makes it unlawful for employers to request polygraph lie-detector tests from employees or job applicants.
- **Worker Adjustment and Retraining Notification Act of 1988 (WARN).** States that employers must give sixty days' warning if they plan to close the plant or lay off workers.
- **Whistleblower Protection Statutes of 1989.** Protects employees of financial institutions and government contractors from retaliating against employees who report violations of the law.
- **Worker Compensation Laws.** Check your state department of labor (see chapter 14) for information on worker compensation issues. Requirements and benefits vary by state.

Benefits

- **Employee Retirement Income Security Act of 1974.** Governs operation of pension and retirement benefits provided by private employers.
- **Family and Medical Leave Act of 1991.** Provides employees of companies with fifty or more employees up to twelve weeks of unpaid, and in some cases paid, leave to care for sick children, relatives, or themselves.

We should also mention the North American Free Trade Agreement (NAFTA). This 1994 agreement among the United States, Canada, and Mexico is designed to reduce or eliminate trade barriers, including tariffs and regulations, among the member nations. The idea is to create a friction-free flow of goods and services among the nations, benefiting each nation in turn. However, NAFTA has caused some companies to face new competition from abroad while strengthening other companies. If you plan on exporting or importing or manufacturing, you might want to research NAFTA to see if it might affect you. Talk to an attorney, federal agencies (SBA and IRS), state agencies, or local chambers of commerce.

As you can see, regulations can be sticky indeed, but if you keep current and get the right advice, you won't get hurt. Whatever you do, don't intentionally break the law just to make a few more dollars. It is not worth the fines, embarrassment, or loss of your company. Make the regulations work for you, and you will have eliminated one of the biggest headaches that businesspeople face.

Figure 11.3: **MAKING COMPLIANCE PUBLIC**

Some of the regulations listed in this chapter must be clearly posted in many places of employment. The minimum wage and the fair employment posters must generally be posted. In some states, others are mandatory.

❑ **Federal and State Minimum Wage**

❑ **Workers Compensation Safety and Fraud Hotline**

❑ **Employee Polygraph Protection Act**

❑ **Job Safety and Health Protection**

❑ **Equal Employment Opportunity Is the Law**

❑ **Family Medical Leave Act**

Your state will have its own list. Again, many of these posters can be obtained at one of the numerous government regulatory bodies or through your state department of labor. Check around.

Federal agencies and websites:

❑ **Small Business Administration: http://www.sba.gov**

❑ **Department of Agriculture: http://www.usda.gov**

❑ **Department of Commerce: http://www.doc.gov**

❑ **Department of Labor: http://www.dol.gov**

❑ **Environmental Protection Agency: http://www.epa.gov**

❑ **U.S. Citizenship and Immigration Services: http://www .uscis.gov/portal/site/uscis**

❑ **Internal Revenue Service: http://www.irs.gov**

❑ **Securities and Exchange Commission: http://www.sec.gov**

Chapter **12**

Planning for Tomorrow

▶ **The business plan versus the strategic plan**

▶ **Examining the strategic plan**

You don't plan a business, flip a switch, and then just run it comfortably until retirement. Being an entrepreneur involves an ongoing process of evaluation and strategic planning beyond, "Well, we kept the lights on again this month!"

Most of the issues we've dealt with in this book have involved putting you in business. Ongoing strategic planning will keep you in business.

After your business is running, you will need to modify your initial business plan to meet current needs. These needs could be growth, contraction, financial changes, or any other of a number of occurrences. At start-up, you need to keep the big picture of economic changes in mind and their potential effect on your business. After start-up, it's all about the ability to sense change and capitalize on what's coming next.

The Business Plan versus the Strategic Plan

The business plan you created for your start-up is the template you'll use to create your first strategic plan and, to a degree, every additional plan you'll make throughout the life of your business. Strategic planning is the process of evaluating and reevaluating processes, products, and goals, and calibrating a vision of your future and the future of your business.

QUICK Tip

Your Future: Why did we say "your future"? Because for many entrepreneurs, outside of family, friends, and home, the business is truly an extension of their lives. That's why strategic planning to a great degree needs to focus on personal goals, which may range from traditional ones like selling or passing down the business so you can retire to planning an end game for the current business and starting another one. In your strategic planning process, you'll definitely want to involve your business attorney and accountant, but you might want to bring in your personal financial adviser or an estate planner as well.

This chapter is designed to introduce you to the concept of strategic planning and to present the many ways that planning can help business growth and profitability.

More worldwide competition, cheaper labor markets, and greater numbers of entrepreneurs starting their own businesses all affect the climate in which you operate. These pressures need to be addressed if your business is to survive.

By regularly addressing them, you will learn to apply proactive and creative solutions to current and upcoming problems. That is the real beauty of strategic planning: it allows you to think effectively about the future. The point here is that you do not want to be eighty years old and still mumbling about what could or should have been. Strategic planning will enable you to do what needs to be done.

Your initial business plan was meant to get your business started and act as a template for future growth—two, three, and five years from start-up and beyond. That initial template may be fine in a general or macro sense, but on the specific or micro level, it will need tweaking. That is where the concept of planning comes into play. Planning will tell you what is right and what is wrong with your small business.

You will learn to recognize those parts of your plan (and goals) that are not working or were unrealistic in the first place. You will certainly come across areas that have either failed to produce the desired results or simply need updating to meet the current state of your business, the economy, or your goals. That's perfectly healthy in a business, but the key is to minimize your weaknesses.

Planning will also highlight your successes and benefit your understanding of what you are doing right. An important part of the ongoing strategic planning is recognizing your strengths and enhancing them. After all, any strength or expertise that becomes apparent is beneficial to your company. You will want to concentrate on exploiting these strengths.

QUICK Tip

Getting an Outside Viewpoint: In the tech industry, many fast-moving companies recruit advisory boards of experienced executives and investors in their field to give the company and its leadership an ongoing critique. Granted, the final decisions are yours, but many business owners operate in isolation, and the sounding-board idea might be a good one for keeping your strategic planning on track.

A strategic plan also enables you to review your short- and long-term goals and understand if these are still realistic milestones to strive for.

Sometimes they must be revised, changed, or eliminated. By planning, you can determine what goals need refinement or elimination. Planning allows you the choice of determining how you will reach these goals on the basis of your current and future business status. It also forces you to examine why those goals were unreachable or why you achieved them.

As we mentioned earlier, all businesses should conduct strategic planning at least once a year. Moreover, SOHO businesses can use strategic planning sessions to facilitate growth, to evaluate the benefits of the home office, and to identify changes or obstacles in the environment. For instance, having a home office is stressful because family and personal life occur everywhere around the office, so you might revise your plan to move into a separate office. Or you may recognize a problem such as a stressed home office and still decide to do nothing about it. In planning your business, you get that choice. Not every problem needs to be addressed, because problems are relative, and their importance to your operations may not warrant any immediate action. When you complete your planning sessions, you will be able to tell where you should expend your efforts.

Sometimes you have to review your progress monthly or quarterly. That's fine. You can fine-tune or adjust your business plan at those times. Also, you can get an earlier glimpse of the success or failure of your strategies. Again, you will be the one to determine when and how you review your strategy implementation.

After you have gone through your initial planning session, you can then use the new strategic plan to rewrite or revise your current business plan. This is useful, especially if you plan growth and need financing. The strategic plan can aid and enhance the business plan, thus making the chances of security financing all the better.

At the end of every year, it's wise to perform a strategic evaluation of your company. If your company is small, the whole staff will probably be involved. If you have grown, the board of directors and top management will want to perform this duty jointly.

FIGURE 12.1: STRATEGIC PLAN OUTLINE

Because a strategic plan is largely a document for your own use, you can decide the structure that will help you the most. Here's an idea of one way to do it. It's wise to create a diary, computer file, or physical file during the year with notes and ideas you want to incorporate into your annual strategic plan revision. You should schedule work time to write it and give yourself an annual deadline to complete it; it's that important.

Suggested Strategic Planning Outline

1. Introduction

- **Executive summary**
  - Top issues in this year's plan
  - Mission statement
  - Current objectives

2. Your Company's Strengths

- **Management and operations**
  - Marketing
  - Finance and accounting

3. Your Company's Weaknesses

- **Management and operations**
  - Marketing
  - Finance and accounting

4. Analysis

- **Competitor analysis**
  - Opportunities for your company

Continued

- Threats to your company

- Summary of issues and actions from last year's strategic plan

5. New Strategic Plan

- **Redefined mission statement**

  - New company objectives

  - Possible strategies

  - Chosen strategies

  - Implementation process

6. Appendixes, Bibliography, Indexes

QUICK Tip

The Four Steps of Strategic Planning: Recognition, formulation, implementation and evaluation (RFIE). Consider this a shortcut for the strategic planning process every time you do it:

- Recognize what happened to your company during the last six months to a year ago.
- Formulate ideas and strategies to enhance your progress and address your problems.
- Implement the strategies and objectives intended to meet new and improved goals
- Set the next date to evaluate these findings and start the process all over again.

Examining the Strategic Plan

Now let's examine each section of this sample strategic plan. At the end of this chapter is a list of SBA publications that might assist you further. One thing to remember is to use this strategic plan to review the work you have done this year and to plan for next year. A plan can help you determine your needs in all areas, including finance. Once this plan is in place, you might set a timetable for borrowing or raising funds through a stock or bond offering. The strategic plan covers a one-year timetable, and it's helpful to keep each plan handy as you develop it year over year as a running history of how you grew, what worked, and what didn't.

QUICK Tip

Keeping Ahead: The best way to stay abreast of current and future trends is to order your competitors' catalogs and products or to try their services on a periodic basis. You'll also need to continuously monitor relevant domestic and foreign events through news magazines, newspapers, and television.

Introduction

The introduction is the front material for your plan and should be completed with as much care as the other four parts of your strategic plan. They will be used to determine new objectives and mission statements.

- Company description: Since the strategic plan is for you, do not include all of the information you already know; instead, you should be covering those things that have changed since your first business plan.
- Issues pertaining to your company: List those economic, political, and social issues at the moment that affect your company directly.
- Mission statement: Write your original mission statement here as a reminder of your basic goals. You might revise it later.
- Current objectives: What are your objectives or goals now? In other words, list your objectives when you wrote your first business plan.

Your Company's Strengths

In the section on company strengths, you will make lists of the positive things that happened to you this year. Your strengths will be self-evident, but listing them will help later when you determine new goals and strategies.

- Management and operations: What, where, and who are your strengths in your company's management? List the things you did right this year. Remember, this strategic plan is for you. Be honest and do not build up your management style or your operations.

- Marketing: Where and what are your marketing strengths? What worked this year? What were the reasons you sold well? What advertising and distribution systems do you credit?
- Finance and accounting: Where and what are your finance and accounting strengths? How did you use your capital to generate business?

Your Company's Weaknesses

Now focus on the negative. Your company's weaknesses are areas in which you recognize what was deficient in your past year and where you need to improve. Weaknesses are important to note because they are the prime areas you will want to focus on to improve your business as quickly and dramatically as possible.

- Management and operations: What, where, and who are your weaknesses in running the company? Why are these things weaknesses? Are you able to keep up with demand?
- Marketing: Where and what are your marketing weaknesses? What marketing and/or advertising did not work? How did your distribution channels suit your business?
- Finance and accounting: Where are your money weaknesses? If you need more capital, note it here. Do your credit policies work? Is there a constant cash flow? Is there any way you can speed up the process?

QUICK Tip

Useful Resources: The SBA publication MP 21, *Introduction to Strategic Planning*, and EB06, *Developing a Strategic Business Plan*, are definitely worth a read.

Analysis

The analysis section analyzes your competitors and how your business stacks up against them. You need to be thorough and honest, because you will use the ideas you generate during this part of the process to consider new strategies.

- Competitor analysis: Who are your competitors and how are they doing? Did they succeed last year? Did they take business away from you?
- Key ingredients matrix: What are the key ingredients for success in your business? List as many factors you can think of.
- Opportunities for your company: Name opportunities forecasted and reported on in various business and news magazines, journals, and programs. These can come from external sources and from inside your company. You should list anything that could help your company.
- Threats to your company: Name events that could threaten or harm your company from various business and news magazines, journals, and programs. Threats can be internal and external. They threaten to reduce sales, profitability, growth, or production.

SWOT Analysis: In a small business atmosphere, your strength will lie in being able to assess your own strengths and weaknesses. SWOT stands for

Strengths
Weaknesses
Opportunities
Threats

New Strategic Plan

Finally, all of the previous analyses come together in this final section to form a cohesive new strategic plan.

First, you will want to compare your strengths and weaknesses alongside your opportunities and threats. This is your SWOT analysis. Next, identify those key ingredients for success that you can maximize through your strengths and opportunities.

Then list your weaknesses and threats and how your strengths and opportunities can help overcome them. Finally, you will want to pick out those areas you specifically want to improve on next year. You do not have to select everything. This will form the basis of your new plan.

- New company objectives: If you need new objectives, formulate them. These new objectives are based on your past objectives and what your SWOT analysis tells you what you need to do next year to improve your business.
- Possible strategies: List as many possible strategies to improve your company as you can think of. Keep in mind that you want to maximize your strengths and opportunities and minimize your weaknesses and threats. Formulate strategies appropriately.
- Chosen strategies: Choose the strategies that you feel will best create the desired outcome and meet the new objectives. Choose only those that you can implement. Some may have to wait until next year. You should address the most urgent needs first.
- Redefined mission statement: If you need a new mission statement after this analysis, write one. Most likely, you will want to enhance the previous one.
- Implementation of chosen strategies: How will you implement the strategies? Make a listing of the ways your strategies can be worked into your operations within your budget. If you are seeking more capital, note this.
- Strategic evaluation: Determine how, over a period of time, you will measure and evaluate the success or failure of your chosen strategies. Once you determine a monthly, quarterly, or yearly evaluation timetable, stick to it.

Appendixes, Bibliography, and Indexes

The section of appendixes, bibliography, and indexes is an optional section to use if you generate supporting documents while working on your strategic plan. If you have an elaborate strategic planning session, you may use this area to file your supporting research and materials.

As you can see, a strategic plan allows you to continuously analyze, update, and revise your two- to five-year business strategy to incorporate changing circumstances, products, or economic forces. This is very, very important. Businesses often fail because of their own shortcomings in the planning department. Even in times of success, you must continuously look over the horizon for future opportunities and threats and behind your back at what your competitors are doing.

Remember: recognize, formulate, implement, and evaluate.

Chapter

13

Resources, Resources

This chapter is your go-to guide for resources to help you plan your business.

As you'll see in chapter 14, resources with incredible depth are moving increasingly to the Internet, and the book you hold in your hand is a good first step to getting there.

What you're about to read is a combination of free and pay resources. We have included government agencies, individuals, and companies that we feel might be of use to you.

Some, like the Small Business Administration, have publications for sale at little or moderate cost—see appendix A for a full list of current titles available for download on the SBA website (http://www.sba.gov). Others, like the Internal Revenue Service, offer their information for free.

Again, some categories will overlap. While this list is by no means exhaustive, it is a good guide of sources available to you.

Books

The first place to look for business books is in your local bookstore. Nearly all bookstores have a dedicated business section, as well as knowledgeable employees who can help you find exactly what you're searching for.

Barnes & Noble's website (http://www.barnesandnoble.com) is a great place to buy books online. Barnes & Noble has hundreds of business titles and business magazines, and it's easy to search for books by category. Other sources to buy books online include independent bookstore websites, Apple's iBookstore, and Amazon. And don't forget about the library!

General
- *Small Business for Dummies*, by Eric Tyson and Jim Schell (Wiley Publishing, 2011). This is the flagship small business book in the Dummies series.
- *The Small Business Handbook*, by Irving Burstiner (Simon and Schuster, 1997). An excellent book for the first timer. Available mostly used online and in libraries.

Start-Ups
- *The $100 Startup: Reinvent the Way You Make a Living, Do What You Love, and Create a New Future*, by Chris Guillebeau (Crown Business, 2012). A best-seller on bootstrapped businesses.
- *Adams Streetwise Small Business Start-Up: Your Comprehensive Guide*

to Starting and Managing a Business, by Bob Adams (Adams Media, 2002). A longtime bible on start-up companies.

Self-Employment
- *Working for Yourself: Law & Taxes for Independent Contractors, Freelancers & Consultants*, by Stephen Fishman (NOLO, 2011). A must-have guide for self-employed workers and freelance contractors.

Business Plan How-Tos
- *Streetwise Complete Business Plan: Writing a Business Plan Has Never Been Easier!*, by Bob Adams (Adams Media, 2002). An in-depth guide to writing your business plan.
- *Your First Business Plan: A Simple Question and Answer Format Designed to Help You Write Your Own Plan*, by Brian Hazelgren and Joseph Covello (Sourcebooks, 2005). A question-and-answer guide to get you jump-started with your business plan.

Franchising
- *The Educated Franchisee: The How-To Book for Choosing a Winning Franchise*, 2nd ed., by Rick Bisio (Bascom Hill, 2011). How to make the most of your franchising opportunity.

Financing
- *How to Get the Financing for Your New Small Business: Innovative Solutions from the Experts Who Do It Every Day*, by Sharon Fullen (Atlantic Publishing, 2006). This book covers traditional and creative financing processes in depth.
- *The SBA Loan Book: The Complete Guide to Getting Financial Help Through the Small Business Administration*, 3rd ed., by Charles H. Green (Adams Media, 2011). This book details the processes for securing SBA loans and provides valuable insight into enhancing your ability to get a loan by revealing the secrets and the dos and don'ts of SBA loan applications.

Government Sources
- **Business.usa.gov.** Also known as BusinessUSA, a spin-off site of http://www.usa.gov that focuses exclusively on small and start-up companies.

- **U.S. Small Business Administration.** Check appendix A; all titles are available for download at http://www.sba.gov. The SBA is specifically geared toward encouraging small business growth and will provide you with most of your information, at least initially. The SBA has publications, videos, software, programs, loans, and websites. The publications, software, and videos are listed in the appendix. The SBA's Small Business Development Centers are located in every state and provide management assistance to current and potential small business owners. Its Business Information Centers are government-private ventures that provide high-tech software and an array of counseling services and training to small businesses. The SBA has field offices are in every major city, as well as Service Corps of Retired Executive (SCORE) centers, which provide small business owners assistance from retired executives and businesspeople. See your state requirements for locations. Also, be sure to get the Small Business Start-Up Kit from the SBA, which is loaded with important information on business start-ups. SBA Answer Desk: 800-827-5722
- **Publications.USA.gov.** The longtime government publications center in Pueblo, Colorado, has moved to the web in a shiny new format at the main site http://publications.usa.gov. Most titles are free, and there's a dedicated small business section on the left-hand menu.
- **Federal Trade Commission.** This organization has more than one hundred free publications on consumer and business topics, including *Consumer Guide to Buying a Franchise*. The best way to access these is by visiting http://www.ftc.gov/bcp/consumer.shtm.
- **Government auctions.** These auctions are excellent ways to get furniture and equipment. Local and federal agencies hold auctions; check your local newspaper for information.
- **Government Printing Office.** This office handles federal documents and publications and has a wealth of information on hundreds of topics, from agriculture to business to history. The best way to get information is to visit the website at http://www.gpo.gov; the catalog search function is at http://catalog.gpo.gov/F?RN=622215013.
- **Internal Revenue Service.** The IRS has dozens of publications. Be sure to get the *Tax Guide for Small Business*. For more information, visit the website http://www.irs.ustreas.gov. The IRS also offers local services like tax seminars and aid programs.
- **Public Libraries.** Of course, you say. But the library is an excellent source of free resources and publications. The librarian will also be

able to assist you in your searches. Your local library should have a business section that will contain guides to such things as trade associations, other companies, services, government information, statistical data, and phone books from other parts of the country.

- **Local Government.** Your local county or city government will likely have an economic development office where you can obtain local assistance and certain SBA loans. Most cities will have local loan, grant, or tax abatement programs such as the urban enterprise zone initiatives.
- **Minority Business Development Agency.** This is the only federal agency created to encourage minority ownership of small businesses. It coordinates federal programs; collects information and dispenses it; and funds training assistance for minorities at nine regional sites in Atlanta, Miami, Chicago, Dallas, New York, Boston, Philadelphia, San Francisco, and Los Angeles. For further information, visit the website at http://www.mbda.gov.

Copyright, Trademark, and Patent Information:

- **U.S. Copyright Office:** Copyrights protect written documents against exploitation. If you produce written materials, works of art, or programs, you will need this information.
  U.S. Copyright Office
  101 Independence Avenue SE
  Washington, DC 20559-6000
  http://www.copyright.gov
  202-707-3000 or 877-476-0778 (toll free)
- **U.S. Trademark and Patent Office:** Where you go to check registered trademarks and patents and begin the process for filing your own.
  U.S. Trademark and Patent Office
  600 Dulany Street
  Madison Buildings (East & West)
  Alexandria, VA
  http://www.uspto.gov
  800-786-9199 (toll-free) or 571-272-1000 (local) or 571-272-9950 (TTY)

Small Business Publications

- **Entrepreneur.com:** Wide-ranging website of *Entrepreneur* magazine.
- **Inc.com:** Companion site to *Inc.* magazine; great coverage of franchise operations.
- **Institute of Management and Administration (http://www.ioma .com):** A website containing e-newsletter listings, business reports, and a management library for research. Note that there is a cost to do certain research, but it might be worth it.

Small Business Tools

- **Wolters Kluwer (CCH):** Now online at http://www.toolkit.com /tools/index.aspx, the longtime Business Owner's Toolkit costs a membership fee of $39 a year with à la carte offerings of detailed legal forms and business books. This company provides publications and information on everything from marketing to employees to business start-ups to aspiring small business owners. Its website at http://www .toolkit.cch.com is excellent and contains many free resources.
  John Duoba
  Publisher and Managing Editor
  Business Owners Toolkit
  2700 Lake Cook Road
  Riverwoods, IL 60015
  customerservice@toolkit.com

News Sites

News junkies might consider following the Twitter sites of these various news organizations—it's like having a real-time news-alert system.
- **Bloomberg.com:** One of the top-rated financial sites on the web, and a great place to follow financial markets, the economy, and interest rates.
- **CNBC.com** and **CNN.com:** Breaking business news online.
- **WSJ.com:** The *Wall Street Journal*'s website, companion to the print product.
- **NYTimes.com:** The *New York Times*, with one of the best national business sections in the nation.
- **Businessinsider.com:** Fast-growing business site.
- ***Nightly Business Report*** on PBS: This program provides an overview

of the day's business and financial news. Some of it directly pertains to small businesses (http://video.pbs.org/program/nbr/)

- **CFO.com:** This site features articles from *CFO* magazine and is useful for keeping abreast of all matters relating to the financial management of any business. Areas of focus include accounting, tax, capital markets, e-commerce, human resources and benefits, and hardware issues, along with top news stories.

Organizations and Groups

- **American Association of Franchisees & Dealers:** This group is a franchise organization that provides information, benefits, publication, and assistance to potential franchisees. Call 800-733-9858, visit their website at http://www.aafd.org, or write to the following address:
  AAFD
  PO Box 81887
  San Diego, CA 92138-1887
- **Better Business Bureau:** These bureaus are in all cities across the nation. The purpose is self-regulation and grievance redress. By joining, you receive the satisfaction that the BBB on your front counter brings. Call your local BBB for information on joining. The BBB also has an online program. Check out the national BBB website at http://www.bbbonline.org.
- **Chambers of Commerce:** Check online for the chamber of commerce in your community. Chambers provide members with localized information, and networking and business opportunities. The chamber will work for your local business area. Membership is a good idea.
- **Direct Marketing Association:** This is a mail-order association that you can join if you plan mail-order sales. It provides services and information that may be of value or use. Check out the website at http://www.newdma.org, or write to the following address:
  DMA
  1120 Avenue of the Americas
  New York, NY 10036
- **International Franchise Association:** This association is similar to the AAFD and will provide information, booklets, and benefits to members. It puts out a publication called *Franchise World*, which is a good place to start your franchise research. Call 202-628-8000, visit their

website at http://www.franchise.org, or write to the following address:
IFA
1350 New York Avenue, NW
Suite 900
Washington, DC 20005-4709

- **National Association for the Self-Employed:** This group publishes two magazines for small business owners, including *Self-Employed America*, and provides information and benefits for members who are usually small business owners. Visit http://www.nase.org or write to the following address:
NASE
PO Box 612067
DFW Airport
Dallas, TX 75261-2067

- **National Association of Women Business Owners:** This group lobbies for women's businesses and has information and services. Visit the website at http://www.nawbo.org or write to the following address:
National Association of Women Business Owners
1595 Spring Hill Road
Suite 330
Vienna, VA 22182

- **National Federation of Independent Businesses:** This group is a lobbying organization for small businesses. It is one of the most powerful small business organizations in the nation. Call 615-872-5800 or 800-NFIB-NOW, visit their website at http://www.nfib.com, or write to the following address:
NFIB
1201 F Street, NW
Suite 200
Washington, DC 20004

- **National Small Business Association:** This is an established business advocate for small businesses. The website is http://www.nsba.org.

This list is by no means exhaustive. Many trade journals and academic journals can be consulted, as can colleges (business and economics professors), government publications and agencies, and private think tanks.

Chapter

14

State-by-State Start-Up Information

▶ **State-by-state resources**

Since the last edition of this book was published, the way state-by-state business start-up information is disseminated to the public has changed substantially, and for the better. Federal, state, and local governments have almost completely turned to the Internet to share critical forms, regulations, and information necessary to business start-ups.

With that knowledge, we are expanding our coverage of public and private resources that prospective business owners can reach by phone, mail, and the Internet.

What if you don't have access to a computer? No worries. Your public library will have Internet access and librarians who can help you find even more localized data than you'll see here.

That said, most general state requirements for business registrations are very similar and follow predictable patterns. In general, unless you plan to operate as a sole proprietor (which is usually the least regulated form of small business, requiring no specific forms to file in many states), you will need to secure a federal Employer Identification Number (EIN), register your business entity with your state and local officials, and obtain state tax registration according to the kind of business and the taxes and fees it must collect. Along the way, you may have to apply for licenses or other permits, including those at the local level.

No matter what kind of business you plan to start, it's very wise to start out working with an attorney, a certified public accountant, and even a financial planner. They'll not only advise you on critical business and tax information necessary to starting your enterprise but also help you customize the structure of your business going forward.

In this chapter you will find the following information for each state:

1. **Secretary of state contact information:** Secretaries of state typically handle all business registration functions, including entity registration (sole proprietorship, partnership, limited liability corporations, and C corporations) and name searches to make sure that your chosen business name is not in conflict with a previously existing business.
2. **Department of Revenue contact information:** Revenue departments handle all tax matters on a statewide basis, although it's also wise to work with tax experts to determine tax responsibilities on a city and county basis.
3. **Department of Labor:** If you are hiring any full- or part-time employees, it's critical to check rules and regulations for work

rule, payroll, and benefits details particular to your state. Again, municipalities and counties may add different requirements to the mix, so check there, too.

4. **State CPA association:** Few people realize how starting a business can complicate both business and personal finances. Even if you are particularly astute on tax matters, it's of critical importance to consult a tax professional before you begin. Your state association can aid in your search.

5. **State bar association:** Most state bar associations run legal referral services. It's always wise to consult an attorney who is specifically familiar with small business start-up issues before you start, not only to make sure the proper papers are filed to start a business but also to help you with business plans and other key strategic issues. If you don't have a personal referral on a good business attorney, state bar associations can be a good start.

QUICK Tip

Employment Law: If you want a great overview of federal employment law, by all means, go to the feds. The U.S. Department of Labor's website features an overview page for all major employment laws enforced on a federal level: http://www.dol.gov/compliance/guide/

6. **Small Business Development Center office:** Each state has an office of this small business assistance network, an offshoot of the U.S. Small Business Administration that partners with local colleges, universities, and state economic development agencies. Each of the approximately one thousand centers offer no-cost business consulting and low-cost training. (Note: Individual states may have more than the one SBDC office listed here; ask for the one nearest you.)

7. **SCORE:** Another offshoot of the U.S. Small Business Administration, the once-named Service Core of Retired Executives is a nonprofit that provides mentoring services to small businesspeople for free and seminars for a fee. (Note: States may have more than the one SCORE office listed here; ask for the one nearest you.)

QUICK Tip

National Business Climate: Interested in the small business climate in all fifty states? The U.S. Small Business Administration's Office of Advocacy has a handy set of descriptions online: http://archive.sba.gov/advo /research/profiles/

For a comparison of tax climates in each state, see appendix B, which compares state-by-state sales, corporate, and individual income tax rates.

State-by-State Resources

Each of these resource lists is subject to change. If you can't find what you're looking for online, follow up by phone, mail, or email (when provided).

Also, in the interest of space, we've listed main contact information for just one office within the agencies listed. Most of these are part of a multilocation system, so check with them to see if they have a location closer to you if you need to visit.

Not all agencies provide email access but we have attempted to include as many public email addresses as possible.

All information, including state-by-state contacts, forms, and requirements, is subject to change.

ALABAMA

Office of the Secretary of State
Office of the Secretary of State
Attn.: Business Services
PO Box 5616
Montgomery, AL 36103-5616
334-242-7200
http://www.sos.state.al.us

Department of Revenue
Alabama Department of Revenue
50 N. Ripley
Montgomery, AL 36132
334-242-1170
http://revenue.alabama.gov

Department of Labor
Alabama Department of Labor
RSA Union, 6th Floor
PO Box 303500
Montgomery, AL 36130-3500
334-242-3460
http://www.alalabor.state.al.us

State CPA Association (CPA Referral)
Alabama Society of Certified Public Accountants
1041 Longfield Court
Montgomery, AL 36117
334-834-7650
http://www.ascpa.org/Public/Referral/FindACPA.aspx

State Bar Association (Attorney Referral)
Alabama State Bar
Lawyer Referral Service
415 Dexter Avenue
Montgomery, AL 36104
800-392-5660
http://www.alabar.org/lrs/
lrs@alabar.org

Small Business Development Center (SBDC) Offices
Alabama SBDC Network
University of Alabama
Box 870396
Tuscaloosa, AL 35487
205-348-1582
http://www.asbdc.org

SCORE Offices
Alabama Capitol SCORE
600 S. Court Street
Montgomery, AL 36104
334-240-6868
http://alabamacapitol.score.org/chapters/alabama-capitol-score

ALASKA

Office of the Secretary of State
Department of Commerce, Community, and Economic Development
Division of Corporations, Business, and Professional Licensing
333 Willoughby Avenue
9th Floor
Juneau, AK 99801-1770
907-465-2550
http://www.commerce.state.ak.us/occ/
corporations@alaska.gov

Department of Revenue
Alaska Department of Revenue
Juneau Commissioner's Office
P.O. Box 110400
333 W. Willoughby, 11th Floor SOB
Juneau, Alaska 99811-0400
907-269-6628
http://www.revenue.state.ak.us
bryan.butcher@alaska.gov

Department of Labor
Alaska Department of Labor and Workforce Development
Commissioner's Office
PO Box 111149
Juneau, AK 99811-1149
907-465-2700
http://labor.state.ak.us/

State CPA Association (CPA Referral)
Alaska Society of CPAs
341 W. Tudor Road, #105
Anchorage, AK 99503
907-562-4334
http://www.akcpa.org

State Bar Association (Attorney Referral)
Alaska Bar Association
550 W. 7th Avenue
Suite 1900
Anchorage, AK 99501
907-272-7469
https://www.alaskabar.org/servlet/content/lawyer_referral_serv.html

Small Business Development Center (SBDC) Offices
Alaska SBDC—State Office
University of Alaska Anchorage
430 W. 7th Avenue
Suite 110
Anchorage, AK 99501
907-274-7232
http://www.aksbdc.org

SCORE Offices
Anchorage SCORE
420 L Street
Suite 300
Anchorage, AK 99501-1971
907-271-4022
http://anchorage.score.org/chapters/anchorage-score

ARIZONA

Office of the Secretary of State
Secretary of State
Capitol Executive Tower
7th Floor
1700 W. Washington Street
Phoenix, AZ 85007-2888
602-542-4285
http://www.azsos.gov/business_services/filings.htm

Department of Revenue
Arizona Department of Revenue
Taxpayer Information & Assistance
PO Box 29086
Phoenix, AZ 85038-9086
800-843-7196
http://www.azdor.gov/Business.aspx

Department of Labor
Department of Labor
800 W. Washington Street
Phoenix AZ 85007
602-542-4411
http://www.ica.state.az.us

State CPA Association (CPA Referral)
Arizona Society of CPAs
4801 E. Washington Street
Suite 225-B
Phoenix, AZ 85034
602-252-4144
https://secure.ascpa.com/find_a_cpa

State Bar Association (Attorney Referral)
State Bar of Arizona
4201 N. 24th St.
Suite 100
Phoenix, AZ 85016-6266
602-252-4804
http://www.azbar.org/FindaLawyer

Small Business Development Center (SBDC) Offices
Arizona SBDC Network
Maricopa County Community Colleges District
2411 W. 14th Street
Suite 114
Tempe, AZ 85281
480-731-8720
http://www.azsbdc.net

SCORE Offices
Greater Phoenix SCORE
2828 N. Central Avenue, #800
Phoenix, AZ 85004
602-745-7250
http://greaterphoenix.score.org/chapters/greater-phoenix-score

ARKANSAS

Office of the Secretary of State
Arkansas Secretary of State
Main Offices
State Capitol, RM 256
Little Rock, AR 72201
501-682-1010
http://www.sos.arkansas.gov/BCS/Pages/default.aspx

Department of Revenue
Department of Finance and Administration
1509 W. 7th Street
Little Rock, AR 72201
501-682-7030
http://www.dfa.arkansas.gov/Pages/businessServices.aspx

Department of Labor
Department of Labor
10421 W. Markham Street
Little Rock, AR 72205
501-682-4500
http://www.labor.ar.gov/Pages/default.aspx
asklabor@arkansas.gov

State CPA Association (CPA Referral)
11300 Executive Center Drive
Little Rock, AR 72211
501-664-8739
http://arcpa.org/content/ascpa-home.aspx
bangel@arcpa.org

State Bar Association (Attorney Referral)
Arkansas Bar Association
2224 Cottondale Lane
Little Rock, AR 72202
800-609-5668
http://www.arkbar.com/pages/find_lawyer.aspx
mglasgow@arkbar.com

Small Business Development Center (SBDC) Offices
Arkansas SBTDC
University of Arkansas at Little Rock
2801 S. University Avenue
Little Rock, AR 72204
501-683-7700
http://asbtdc.org

SCORE Offices
Little Rock SCORE
2120 Riverfront Drive Suite 250
Little Rock, AR 72202
501-324-7379, ext. 302
http://littlerock.score.org/chapters/little-rock-score-0

CALIFORNIA

Office of the Secretary of State
Secretary of State
1500 11th Street
Sacramento, CA 95814
916-653-6814
http://www.sos.ca.gov/business/

Franchise Tax Board
Franchise Tax Board
3321 Power Inn Road
Suite 250
Sacramento, CA 95826-3893
800-852-5711
https://www.ftb.ca.gov/businesses/index.shtml?WT.mc_id=Global
_Businesses_Tab

Department of Labor
California Labor & Workforce Development Agency
800 Capitol Mall, MIC-55
Sacramento, CA 95814
916-653-9900
http://www.labor.ca.gov

State CPA Association (CPA Referral)
CalCPA
1800 Gateway Drive
Suite 200
San Mateo, CA 94404-4072
800-922-5272
http://www.calcpa.org/public/referral/findcpa.aspx

State Bar Association (Attorney Referral)
State Bar of California
180 Howard Street
San Francisco, CA 94105
415-538-2000
http://members.calbar.ca.gov/fal/MemberSearch/FindLegalHelp

Small Business Development Center (SBDC) Offices
Northern California Regional SBDC
Humboldt State University
1 Harpst Street
House 71
Arcata, CA 95521
707-826-3919
http://www.norcalsbdc.org

SCORE Offices
Sacramento SCORE
4990 Stockton Boulevard
Sacramento, CA 95820
916-635-9085
http://sacramento.score.org/chapters/sacramento-score

COLORADO

Office of the Secretary of State
Office of the Secretary of State
1700 Broadway
Denver, CO 80290
303-894-2200, press 2
http://www.sos.state.co.us

Department of Revenue
Colorado Department of Revenue
1375 Sherman Street
Denver, CO 80261
303-866-5610
http://www.colorado.gov/cs/Satellite/Revenue/REVX/1251570868469

Department of Labor
Department of Labor and Employment
633 17th Street
Suite 200
Denver, CO 80202-3611
303-318-8441
http://www.colorado.gov/cs/Satellite/CDLE-Main
/CDLE/1240336821467

State CPA Association (CPA Referral)
Colorado Society of Certified Public Accountants
7979 E. Tufts Avenue
Suite 1000
Denver, CO 80237-2847
800-523-9082
http://www.cocpa.org/for-the-public/find-cpa.html

State Bar Association (Attorney Referral)
Colorado Bar Association
1900 Grant Street
9th Floor
Denver, CO 80203
303-860-1115
http://www.cobar.org/directory/index.cfm?ID=20036

Small Business Development Center (SBDC) offices
Colorado SBDC/Colorado Office of Economic Development and
International Trade
1625 Broadway
Suite 2700
Denver, CO 80202
303-892-3864
http://www.advancecolorado.com

SCORE Offices
SCORE Denver
721 19th Street
Room 426
Denver, CO 80202
303-844-3985
http://denver.score.org/chapters/score-denver

CONNECTICUT

Office of the Secretary of State
Office of the Secretary of the State
State of Connecticut
30 Trinity Street
Hartford, CT 06106
860-509-6200
http://www.sots.ct.gov/sots/site/default.asp

Department of Revenue

Department of Revenue Services
25 Sigourney Street
Suite 2
Hartford, CT 06106-5032
860-297-5962
http://www.ct.gov/drs/site/default.asp

Department of Labor

Connecticut Department of Labor
200 Folly Brook Boulevard
Wethersfield, CT 06109
860-263-6000
http://www.ctdol.state.ct.us/gendocs/employers.html

State CPA Association (CPA Referral)

Connecticut Society of CPAs
716 Brook Street
Suite 100
Rocky Hill, CT
860-258-0214
http://www.ctcpas.org/public/referral/findcpa.aspx

State Bar Association (Attorney Referral)

Connecticut Bar Association
30 Bank Street
PO Box 350
New Britain, CT 06050-0350
860-223-4400
https://www.ctbar.org/Information%20For/Public.aspx

Small Business Development Center (SBDC) Offices
Connecticut Small Business Development Center
Central Connecticut State University
185 Main Street
New Britain, CT 06051
855-702-3279
http://www.ccsu.edu/sbdc

SCORE Offices
Greater Hartford SCORE
330 Main Street
2nd Floor
Hartford, CT 06106
860-240-4700
http://greaterhartford.score.org/chapters/greater-hartford-score

DELAWARE

Office of the Secretary of State
Division of Corporations
John G. Townsend Building
401 Federal Street
Suite 4
Dover, DE 19901
302-739-3073, press 2
http://corp.delaware.gov

Department of Revenue
Department of Finance, Division of Revenue
Carvel State Office Building
820 N. French Street
Wilmington, DE 19801
302-577-8205
http://revenue.delaware.gov/services/BusServices.shtml

Department of Labor
Delaware Department of Labor
4425 N. Market Street
Wilmington, DE 19802
302-761-8085
http://www.delawareworks.com

State CPA Association (CPA Referral)
Delaware Society of Certified Public Accountants
3512 Silverside Road
8 The Commons
Wilmington, DE 19810
302-478-7442
http://www.dscpa.org/find_a_cpa/

State Bar Association (Attorney Referral)
Delaware State Bar Association
301 N. Market Street
Wilmington, DE 19801
302-658-5279
http://www.dvls.org/LRS_Public.htm

Small Business Development Center (SBDC) Offices
Delaware SBTDC
Delaware Technology Park
1 Innovation Way
Suite 301
Newark, DE 19711
302-831-1555
http://www.dsbtdc.org

SCORE Offices
Delaware SCORE
1007 Orange Street
Nemours Building, Suite 1120
Wilmington, DE 19801
302-573-6552
http://delaware.score.org/chapters/delaware-score

FLORIDA

Office of the Secretary of State
Department of State, Division of Corporations
Clifton Building
2661 Executive Center Circle
Tallahassee, FL 32301
850-245-6052
http://www.sunbiz.org
corphelp@dos.state.fl.us

Department of Revenue
Florida Department of Revenue
5050 W. Tennessee Street
Tallahassee, FL 32399-0100
850-617-8600
http://dor.myflorida.com/dor/info_business.html

Department of Labor
866-693-6748
http://www.workforceflorida.com/

State CPA Association (CPA Referral)
Florida Institute of CPAs
325 W. College Avenue
Tallahassee, FL 32301
800-342-3197
http://www.ficpa.org/public/referral/findcpa.aspx

State Bar Association (Attorney Referral)
Florida Bar
651 E. Jefferson Street
Tallahassee, FL 32399-2300
850-561-5600
http://www.floridabar.org/tfb/TFBConsum.nsf/48E76203493B82AD8
52567090070C9B9/EC2322E512B83D1E85256B2F006CC812?Open
Document

Small Business Development Center (SBDC) Offices
Florida SBDC Network
University of West Florida
11000 University Parkway, Building 38
Pensacola, FL 32514
850-473-7801
http://www.FloridaSBDC.org

SCORE Offices
Broward SCORE
299 E. Broward Boulevard
Ft. Lauderdale, FL 33301
954-356-7263
http://broward.score.org/chapters/broward-score

GEORGIA

Office of the Secretary of State
Georgia Secretary of State
2 MLK Jr. Drive
Suite 313
Floyd West Tower
Atlanta, GA 30334-1530
404-656-2817
http://www.sos.ga.gov/corporations/

Department of Revenue
Department of Revenue
1800 Century Boulevard
Atlanta, GA 30345
404-417-2100
https://etax.dor.ga.gov

Department of Labor
Department of Labor
Sussex Place, Room 600
148 Andrew Young International Boulevard, NE
Atlanta, GA 30303
404-232-7300
http://www.dol.state.ga.us/em/

State CPA Association (CPA Referral)
Georgia Society of CPAs
3353 Peachtree Road NE
Suite 400
Atlanta, GA 30326-1414
404-231-8676
http://www.gscpa.org/Content/Consumers.aspx

State Bar Association (Attorney Referral)
State Bar of Georgia
104 Marietta Street NW
Suite 100
Atlanta, GA 30303
404-527-8700
http://www.gabar.org

Small Business Development Center (SBDC) Offices
Georgia SBDC Network State Office
University of Georgia
1180 E. Broad Street
Athens, GA 30602
706-542-2762
http://www.georgiasbdc.org

SCORE Offices
Atlanta SCORE
233 Peachtree Street NE
Harris Tower, Suite 1900
Atlanta, GA 30303
404-331-0121
http://atlanta.score.org/chapters/atlanta-score

HAWAII

Office of the Secretary of State
Department of Commerce and Consumer Affairs
Business Registration Division
PO Box 40
Honolulu, HI 96810
808-586-2744
http://hawaii.gov/dcca/breg

Department of Taxation
State of Hawaii Department of Taxation
PO Box 259
Honolulu, HI 96809-0259
808-587-4242
http://www.state.hi.us/tax/tax.html

Department of Labor
Department of Labor & Industrial Relations
830 Punchbowl Street
Honolulu, HI 96813
808-586-8970
http://hawaii.gov/labor/
dlir.ui.honolulu@hawaii.gov

State CPA Association (CPA Referral)
Hawaii Society of Certified Public Accountants
900 Fort Street Mall
Suite 850
Honolulu, HI 96813
808-537-9475
http://www.hscpa.org/find_a_cpa/index.php

State Bar Association (Attorney Referral)
Alakea Corporate Tower
1100 Alakea Street
Suite 1000
Honolulu, HI 96813
808-537-1868
http://www.hsba.org/Find_a_lawyer.aspx

Small Business Development Center (SBDC) Offices
Hawai'i SBDC Network
308 Kamehameha Avenue Suite 201
Hilo, HI 96720
808-974-7515
http://www.hisbdc.org

SCORE Offices
SCORE of Hawaii
500 Ala Moana Boulevard
Suite 1-306A
Honolulu, HI 96813
808-547-2700
http://hawaii.score.org/chapters/score-hawaii

IDAHO

Office of the Secretary of State
Idaho Secretary of State
PO Box 83720
Boise, ID 83720-0080
208-334-2300
http://www.sos.idaho.gov/corp/corindex.htm

Department of Revenue
Idaho State Tax Commission
PO Box 36
Boise, ID 83722-0410
800-972-7660
http://tax.idaho.gov/p-businesses.cfm

Department of Labor
Department of Labor
317 W. Main Street
Boise, ID 83735-0001
208-332-3570
http://labor.idaho.gov/dnn/Default.aspx?alias=labor.idaho.gov/dnn/idl

State CPA Association (CPA Referral)
Idaho Society of Certified Public Accountants
1649 W. Shoreline Drive
Suite 202
Boise, ID 83702
208-344-6261
http://www.idcpa.org/Locator/Locator.aspx

State Bar Association (Attorney Referral)
Idaho State Bar
525 W. Jefferson Street
Boise, ID 83702
208-334-4500
http://isb.idaho.gov/general/findattorney.html

Small Business Development Center (SBDC) Offices
Idaho SBDC
Boise State University
1910 University Drive
Boise, ID 83725
208-426-3799
http://www.idahosbdc.org

SCORE Offices
Eastern Idaho SCORE
2300 N. Yellowstone Hwy
Suite 119
Idaho Falls, ID 83401
208-523-1022
http://easternidaho.score.org/chapters/eastern-idaho-score

ILLINOIS

Office of the Secretary of State
Secretary of State
Michael J. Howlett Building
501 S. Second Street
Room 350
Springfield, IL 62756
217-785-3000
http://www.cyberdriveillinois.com/departments/business_services
/home.html

Department of Revenue
Willard Ice Building
101 W. Jefferson Street
Springfield, IL 62702
800-732-8866
http://www.revenue.state.il.us/Businesses/

Department of Labor
Illinois Department of Labor
900 S. Spring Street
Springfield, IL 62704
217-782-6206
http://www.state.il.us/agency/idol/

State CPA Association (CPA Referral)
Illinois CPA Society
550 W. Jackson
Suite 900
Chicago, IL 60661
312-993-0407
http://www.icpas.org/hc-consumers.aspx?id=404

State Bar Association (Attorney Referral)
Illinois Bar Center
424 S. Second Street
Springfield, IL 62701-1779
217-525-1760
http://www.illinoislawyerfinder.com

Small Business Development Center (SBDC) Offices
Illinois SBDC
Department of Commerce and Economic Opportunity
500 E. Monroe Street
5th Floor
Springfield, IL 62701
800-252-2923
http://www.ildceo.net/dceo/Bureaus/Entrepreneurship+and+Small+Bu
siness/sbdc.htm

SCORE Offices
Springfield SCORE
3330 Ginger Creek Drive
Suite B South
Springfield, IL 62711
217-793-5020
http://springfieldil.score.org/chapters/springfield-score

INDIANA

Office of the Secretary of State
Office of the Indiana Secretary of State
200 W. Washington Street
Room 201
Indianapolis, IN 46204
317-232-6531
http://www.in.gov/business.htm

Department of Revenue
Indiana Department of Revenue
Re: Sales Tax
PO Box 6195
Indianapolis, IN 46206-0040
317-232-0129
http://www.in.gov/core/business.html

Department of Labor
Department of Labor
Indiana Government Center South
402 W. Washington Street
Room W195
Indianapolis, IN 46204
317-232-2655
http://www.in.gov/core/business.html

State CPA Association (CPA Referral)
Indiana CPA Society
8250 Woodfield Crossing Boulevard #100
Indianapolis, IN 46240-4348
317-726-5000
http://incpas.org/Public/professional/find-a-cpa.aspx

State Bar Association (Attorney Referral)
Indiana State Bar Association
One Indiana Square
Suite 530
Indianapolis, IN 46204
317-639-5465
http://www.inbar.org/Home/tabid/36/Default.aspx

Small Business Development Center (SBDC) Offices
Indiana SBDC
One North Capitol Avenue
Suite 700
Indianapolis, IN 46204
317-232-8805
http://www.isbdc.org

SCORE Offices
Indianapolis SCORE
8500 Keystone Crossing
Suite 401
Indianapolis, IN 46240
317-226-7264
http://indianapolis.score.org/chapters/indianapolis

IOWA

Office of the Secretary of State
Secretary of State
Lucas Building, First Floor
321 E. 12th Street
Des Moines, IA 50319
515-281-5204
http://sos.iowa.gov/business/FormsAndFees.html
sos@sos.iowa.gov

Department of Revenue
Iowa Department of Revenue
Hoover State Office Building
1305 E. Walnut
Des Moines, IA 50319
515-281-3114
http://www.iowa.gov/tax/index.html

Department of Labor
Iowa Labor Services Division
1000 E. Grand Avenue
Des Moines, IA 50319-0209
515-281-5387
http://www.iowaworkforce.org/labor/

State CPA Association (CPA Referral)
Iowa Society of Certified Public Accountants
950 Office Park Road
Suite 300
West Des Moines, IA 50265-2548
515-223-8161
https://www.iacpa.org/Resources/FindACPA.aspx

State Bar Association (Attorney Referral)
Iowa Bar Headquarters
625 E. Court Avenue
Des Moines, IA 50309
515-243-3179
http://www.iabar.net/AttorneyOnLine.nsf/srch

Small Business Development Center (SBDC) Offices
Iowa SBDC
Iowa State University
2321 N. Loop Drive
Suite 202
Ames, IA 50010
515-294-2030
http://www.iowasbdc.org

SCORE Offices
Iowa City SCORE
PO Box 1853
Iowa City, IA 52240
319-338-1662
http://iowacity.score.org/chapters/iowa-city-score

KANSAS

Office of the Secretary of State
Kansas Secretary of State
Memorial Hall, 1st Floor
120 SW 10th Avenue
Topeka, KS 66612-1594
785-296-4564
http://www.kssos.org/business/business.html

Department of Revenue
Kansas Department of Revenue
915 SW Harrison Street
Topeka, KS 66699-3000
785-296-3909
http://www.ksrevenue.org/business.html

Department of Labor
Department of Labor
401 SW Topeka Boulevard
Topeka, KS 66603-3182
785-296-5000
http://www.dol.ks.gov

State CPA Association (CPA Referral)
Kansas Society of Certified Public Accountants
100 SE 9th Street
Suite 502
Topeka, KS 66612-1213
785-272-4366
http://www.kscpa.org/for_the_public/find_a_cpa

State Bar Association (Attorney Referral)
Kansas Bar Association
1200 SW Harrison Street
Topeka, KS 66612-1806
785-234-5696
https://m360.ksbar.org/frontend/search.aspx?cs=3602

Small Business Development Center (SBDC) Offices
Kansas SBDC
214 SW 6th Street
Suite 301
Topeka, KS 66603
785-296-6514
http://ksbdc.kansas.gov/Pages/default.aspx

SCORE Offices
Topeka SCORE
120 SE 6th Avenue
Suite 110
Topeka, KS 66603
785-234-3049
http://topeka.score.org/chapters/topeka-score

KENTUCKY

Office of the Secretary of State
Office of the Secretary of State
Capitol Building
700 Capital Avenue
Suite 152
Frankfort, KY 40601
502-564-3490
http://sos.ky.gov/forms.htm

Department of Revenue
Kentucky Department of Revenue
Frankfort, KY 40602
502-564-4581
http://revenue.ky.gov/business/

Department of Labor
Kentucky Labor Cabinet
1047 U.S. Highway 127 S.
Suite 4
Frankfort, KY 40601-4381
502-564-3070
http://www.labor.ky.gov/Pages/LaborHome.aspx

State CPA Association (CPA Referral)
Kentucky Society of CPAs
1735 Alliant Avenue
Louisville, KY 40299
502-266-5272
http://www.kycpa.org/cpa_referral/referralservice.asp

State Bar Association (Attorney Referral)
Kentucky Bar Association
514 W. Main Street
Frankfort KY 40601-1812
502-564-3795
http://www.kybar.org

Small Business Development Center (SBDC) Offices
Kentucky SBDC
University of Kentucky
1 Quality Street
Suite 635
Lexington, KY 40507
859-257-7668
http://ksbdc.org

SCORE Offices
Louisville SCORE
600 Dr. Martin Luther King Jr. Place Federal Office Building
Room 188
Louisville, KY 40202
502-582-5976
http://louisville.score.org/chapters/louisville-score

LOUISIANA

Office of the Secretary of State
Louisiana Secretary of State
PO Box 94125
Baton Rouge, LA 70804-9125
225-925-4704
http://www.sos.la.gov/tabid/66/Default.aspx

Department of Revenue
Department of Revenue
PO Box 201
Baton Rouge, LA 70821
225-219-7462
http://www.revenue.louisiana.gov/sections/business/default.aspx

Department of Labor
Louisiana Workforce Commission
1001 N. 23rd Street
Baton Rouge, LA 70802-9094
225-342-3111
http://www.laworks.net

State CPA Association (CPA Referral)
Society of Louisiana Certified Public Accountants
2400 Veterans Boulevard
Suite 500
Kenner, LA 70062
504-464-1040
http://www.lcpa.org

State Bar Association (Attorney Referral)
Louisiana State Bar Association
601 St. Charles Avenue
New Orleans, LA 70130-3404
504-566-1600
http://www.lsba.org/MembershipDirectory
/LawyerReferralInformation.asp?Menu=PR

Small Business Development Center (SBDC) Offices
Louisiana SBDC
700 University Avenue
George T. Walker Hall 2-101
Monroe, LA 71209
318-342-5506
http://www.lsbdc.org

SCORE Offices
Baton Rouge SCORE
7117 Florida Boulevard
Louisiana Technology Park, Suite 313
Baton Rouge, LA 70806
225-381-7130
http://batonrougearea.score.org/chapters/baton-rouge-area-score

MAINE

Office of the Secretary of State
Secretary of State
101 State House Station
Augusta, Maine 04333-0101
207-624-7736 and 207-624-9670
http://www.maine.gov/sos/cec/corp/smallbusiness.html

Department of Revenue
Department of Revenue
PO Box 9107
Augusta, ME 04332-9107
207-624-9670
http://www.state.me.us/revenue/
corporate.tax@maine.gov

Department of Labor
Department of Labor
54 State House Station Drive
Augusta, ME 04333
207-623-7900
http://www.state.me.us/labor/

State CPA Association (CPA Referral)
Maine Society of Certified Public Accountants
153 US Route 1
Suite 8
Scarborough, ME 04074-9053
207-883-6090
http://www.mecpa.org

State Bar Association (Attorney Referral)
Maine State Bar Association
124 State Street
Augusta, ME 04330
207-622-7523
http://www.mainebar.org/public_lris.asp
info@mainebar.org

Small Business Development Center (SBDC) Offices
Maine SBDC
University of Southern Maine School of Business
96 Falmouth Street
Portland, ME 04104
207-780-4420
http://www.mainesbdc.org

SCORE Offices
Augusta SCORE
68 Sewall Street
Room 512
Augusta, ME 04330
207-622-8509
http://augustame.score.org/chapters/augusta-score

MARYLAND

Office of the Secretary of State
16 Francis Street
Annapolis, MD 21401
410-974-5521
http://www.sos.state.md.us

Department of Revenue
State Office Building
301 W. Preston Street
Room 206
Baltimore, MD 21201-2384
410-767-1995
http://business.marylandtaxes.com

Department of Labor
Department of Labor, Licensing, and Regulation
500 N. Calvert Street
Suite 401
Baltimore, MD 21202
410-230-6001
http://www.dllr.state.md.us

State CPA Association (CPA Referral)
Maryland Association of CPAs
901 Dulaney Valley Road
Suite 710
Towson, MD 21204-2683
800-782-2036
http://www.macpa.org/public/referral/findcpa.aspx

State Bar Association (Attorney Referral)
Maryland State Bar Association
520 W. Fayette Street
Baltimore, MD 21201
410-685-7878
http://www.msba.org/public/referral.asp

Small Business Development Center (SBDC) Offices
Maryland SBDC
7100 Baltimore Avenue
Suite 401
College Park, MD 20740
301-403-8300, ext. 15
http://www.mdsbdc.umd.edu

SCORE Offices
Greater Baltimore SCORE
10 S. Howard Street
City Crescent Building, 6th Floor
Baltimore, MD 21201
410-962-2233
http://greaterbaltimore.score.org/chapters/greater-baltimore-score

MASSACHUSETTS

Office of the Secretary of State
Secretary of the Commonwealth
One Ashburton Place, 17th Floor
Boston, MA 02108
617-727-9640
http://www.sec.state.ma.us/cor/coridx.htm

Department of Revenue
Massachusetts Department of Revenue
PO Box 7010
Boston, MA 02204
617-887-6367
http://www.mass.gov/dor/businesses/

Department of Labor
Executive Office of Labor & Workforce Development
One Ashburton Place, Room 2112
Boston, MA 02108
617-626-7122
http://www.mass.gov/lwd/

State CPA Association (CPA Referral)
Massachusetts Society of Certified Public Accountants
105 Chauncy Street
10th Floor
Boston, MA 02111
800-392-6145
http://www.mscpaonline.org/consumer/find_a_cpa/
mscpa@MSCPAonline.org

State Bar Association (Attorney Referral)
MBA Boston Office
20 West Street
Boston, MA 02111-1204
617-338-0500
http://www.massbar.org/for-the-public/need-a-lawyer

Small Business Development Center (SBDC) Offices
MSBDC State Office
227 Isenberg School of Management
UMass
121 Presidents Drive
Amherst, MA 01003
413-545-6301
http://www.msbdc.org

SCORE Offices
Boston SCORE
10 Causeway Street
Boston, MA 02222
617-565-5591
http://boston.score.org/chapters/boston-score

MICHIGAN

Department of Licensing and Regulatory Affairs
PO Box 30004
Lansing, MI 48909
517-373-1820
http://www.michigan.gov/lara/0,4601,7-154-35299_61343_35413
---,00.html
LARAcom@michigan.gov

Department of Revenue
Michigan Department of Treasury
Lansing, MI 48922
517-636-6925
http://www.michigan.gov/business
treasReg@michigan.gov

Department of Labor
Department of Licensing & Regulatory Affairs
611 W. Ottawa
PO Box 30004
Lansing, MI 48909
517-373-1820
http://www.michigan.gov/lara/0,4601,7-154-61256---,00.html

State CPA Association (CPA Referral)
Michigan Association of Certified Public Accountants
5480 Corporate Drive
Suite 200
Troy, MI 48098-2642
248-267-3700
http://www.michcpa.org/Aptify/Referral/FindCPA.aspx
macpa@michcpa.org

State Bar Association (Attorney Referral)
State Bar of Michigan
Michael Franck Building
306 Townsend Street
Lansing, MI 48933-2012
517-346-6300
http://www.michbar.org/programs/lawyerreferral.cfm

Small Business Development Center (SBDC) Offices
Michigan SBTDC
State Director
510 W. Fulton Street
Grand Rapids, MI 49504
616-331-7480
http://misbtdc.org

SCORE Offices
Detroit SCORE
477 Michigan Avenue
Suite 515
Detroit, MI 48226
313-226-7947
http://detroit.score.org/chapters/detroit-score

MINNESOTA

Office of the Secretary of State
Office of the Secretary of State
Retirement Systems of Minnesota Building
60 Empire Drive
Suite 100
St Paul, MN 55103
651-296-2803
http://www.sos.state.mn.us/index.aspx?page=3

Department of Revenue
Minnesota Department of Revenue
600 N. Robert Street
St. Paul, MN 55101
651-556-3000
http://www.revenue.state.mn.us/businesses/Pages/Tax-Types.aspx

State CPA Association (CPA Referral)
Minnesota Society of Certified Public Accountants
1650 W. 82nd Street
Suite 600
Bloomington, MN 55431
952-831-2707
http://www.mncpa.org/find-a-cpa/

State Bar Association (Attorney Referral)
Minnesota State Bar Association
600 Nicollet Mall, #380
Minneapolis, MN 55402
612-333-1183
http://www.mnbar.org/nav-find.asp

Small Business Development Center (SBDC) Offices
Minnesota SBDC State Office
Minnesota Department of Employment and Economic Development
332 Minnesota Street
Suite E200
St. Paul, MN 55101
651-259-7423
http://www.positivelyminnesota.com/Business/index.aspx

SCORE Offices
Minneapolis SCORE
8800 Minnesota 7 Bremer Bank Building
St. Louis Park, MN 55426
952-938-4570
http://minneapolis.score.org/chapters/minneapolis-score

MISSISSIPPI

Office of the Secretary of State
Secretary of State
700 North Street
PO Box 136
Jackson, MS 39205-0136
601-359-1633
http://www.sos.ms.gov/business_services.aspx

Department of Revenue
Mississippi Department of Revenue
PO Box 1033
Jackson, MS 39215-1033
601-923-7000
http://www.dor.ms.gov/business.html

Department of Labor
Department of Employment Security
1235 Echelon Parkway
PO Box 1699
Jackson, MS 39215-1699
601-321-6000
http://www.mdes.ms.gov/Home/EmployerServices/index.html

State CPA Association (CPA Referral)
Mississippi Society of Certified Public Accountants
306 Southampton Row
The Commons
Highland Colony Parkway
Ridgeland, MS 39157
601-856-4244
http://www.ms-cpa.org/find.asp

State Bar Association (Attorney Referral)
Mississippi Bar
PO Box 2168
Jackson, MS 39225-2168
601-948-4471
http://www.msbar.org

Small Business Development Center (SBDC) Offices
Mississippi SBDC
122 Jeanette Phillips Drive
PO Box 1848
University, MS 38677
662-915-5001
http://www.mssbdc.org

SCORE Offices
Gulfcoast SCORE
2510 14th Street Hancock Bank
Suite 105
Gulfport, MS 39501
228-875-0691
http://gulfcoast.score.org/chapters/gulfcoast-score

MISSOURI

Office of the Secretary of State
Missouri Secretary of State
600 W. Main Street
Jefferson City, MO 65101
573-751-4936
http://www.sos.mo.gov/categories.asp?id=2

Department of Revenue
Harry S. Truman State Office Building
301 W. High Street
Jefferson City, MO 65101
573-751-3505
http://dor.mo.gov/business/

Department of Labor
Labor and Industrial Relations Commission
PO Box 504
421 E. Dunklin
Jefferson City, MO 65102-0504
573-751-2461
http://www.labor.mo.gov

State CPA Association (CPA Referral)
Missouri Society of Certified Public Accountants
PO Box 419042
St. Louis, MO 63141-9042
314-997-7966
http://www.mocpa.org

State Bar Association (Attorney Referral)
Missouri Bar
326 Monroe
PO Box 119
Jefferson City, MO 65102-0119
573-635-4128
http://www.mobar.org/lrs/clients.htm

Small Business Development Center (SBDC) Offices
Missouri SBTDC
University of Missouri–Columbia
410 S. 6th Street, 200 Engineering North
Columbia, MO 65211
573-884-1555
http://www.missouribusiness.net

SCORE Offices
Springfield Missouri SCORE
830 E. Primrose Street
Suite 101
Springfield, MO 65807
417-890-8501
http://springfieldmo.score.org/chapters/springfield-missouri-score

MONTANA

Office of the Secretary of State
Secretary of State
State Capitol Building
1301 E. 6th Avenue
Helena, MT 59601
406-444-2034
http://sos.mt.gov/Business/index.asp

Department of Revenue
Sam W. Mitchell Building
125 N. Roberts
3rd Floor
Helena, MT 59601
866-859-2254
http://revenue.mt.gov/forbusinesses/default.mcpx

Department of Labor
Department of Labor and Industry
PO Box 1728
Helena, MT 59624-1728
406-444-2840
http://www.dli.mt.gov

State CPA Association (CPA Referral)
Montana Society of Certified Public Accountants
33 S. Last Chance Gulch, Suite 2B
Helena, MT 59601
406-442-7301
https://www.mscpa.org/find_a_cpa

State Bar Association (Attorney Referral)
State Bar of Montana
7 W. 6th Avenue, Suite 2B
PO Box 577
Helena, MT 59624
406-442-7660
https://m360.montanabar.org/frontend/search.aspx?cs=41

Small Business Development Center (SBDC) Offices
Montana SBDC
301 S. Park Avenue
Room 116
Helena, MT 59620
406-841-2746
http://sbdc.mt.gov/default.mcpx

SCORE Offices
Helena SCORE
10 W. 15th Street
Suite 1100
Helena, MT 59626
406-441-1081
http://helena.score.org/chapters/helena-score

NEBRASKA

Office of the Secretary of State
Nebraska Secretary of State
PO Box 94608
Lincoln, NE 68509-4608
402-471-4079
http://www.sos.ne.gov/business/corp_serv/index.html

Department of Revenue
Nebraska State Office Building
301 Centennial Mall South
2nd Floor
PO Box 94818
Lincoln, NE 68509-4818
402-471-5729
http://www.revenue.state.ne.us/index.html

Department of Labor
Department of Labor
550 S. 16th Street
Lincoln, NE 68508
402-471-9000
http://www.dol.nebraska.gov

State CPA Association (CPA Referral)
Nebraska Society of CPAs
635 S. 14th Street
Suite 330
Lincoln, NE 68508
402-476-8482
http://www.nescpa.org
society@nescpa.org

State Bar Association (Attorney Referral)
Nebraska State Bar Association
635 S. 14th Street
Suite 200
PO Box 81809
Lincoln, NE 68508
402-475-7091
http://nebar.com/displaycommon.cfm?an=1&subarticlenbr=151

Small Business Development Center (SBDC) Offices
Nebraska Business Development Center
University of Nebraska at Omaha
Mammel Hall
Suite 200
6708 Pine Street
Omaha, NE 68182
402-554-2521
http://nbdc.unomaha.edu

SCORE Offices
Lincoln SCORE
285 S. 68th Place
Suite 530
Lincoln, NE 68510
402-437-2409
http://lincoln.score.org/chapters/lincoln-score

NEVADA

Office of the Secretary of State
Secretary of State
Nevada State Capitol Building
101 N. Carson Street
Suite 3
Carson City, NV 89701
775-684-5708
http://nvsos.gov/index.aspx?page=4

Department of Revenue
Nevada Department of Taxation
1550 College Parkway
Carson City, NV 89706
775-684-2000
http://tax.state.nv.us

Department of Labor
Office of the Labor Commissioner
555 E. Washington Avenue
Suite 4100
Las Vegas, NV 89101-1050
702-486-2650
http://www.laborcommissioner.com

State CPA Association (CPA Referral)
Nevada Society of Certified Public Accountants
750 Sandhill Road
Suite 120
Reno, NV 89521
775-826-6800
http://members.nevadacpa.org/imispublic/core/referral.aspx
nscpa@nevadacpa.org

State Bar Association (Attorney Referral)
State Bar of Nevada
600 E. Charleston Boulevard
Las Vegas, NV 89104
702-382-2200
http://www.nvbar.org/content/lris-online-referral-request

Small Business Development Center (SBDC) Offices
Nevada SBDC
UNR Campus, Ansari Business Building
Room 411
Reno, NV 89557
775-784-1717
http://nsbdc.org

SCORE Offices
Southern Nevada SCORE
400 S. 4th Street
Suite 250
Las Vegas, NV 89101
702-388-6104
http://southernnevada.score.org/chapters/southern-nevada-score

NEW HAMPSHIRE

Office of the Secretary of State
Corporation Division
NH Department of State
107 N. Main Street
Concord, NH 03301-4989
603-271-3246
http://sos.nh.gov/Corp_Div.aspx

Department of Revenue
Department of Revenue Administration
109 Pleasant Street
Concord, NH 03301
603-230-5000
http://www.revenue.nh.gov/index.htm

Department of Labor
Department of Labor
State Office Park South
95 Pleasant Street
Concord, NH 03301
603-271-3176
http://www.labor.state.nh.us

State CPA Association (CPA Referral)
New Hampshire Society of CPAs
1750 Elm Street
Suite 403
Manchester, NH 03104
603-622-1999
http://www.nhscpa.org/find_a_cpa/

State Bar Association (Attorney Referral)
New Hampshire Bar Association
2 Pillsbury Street
Suite 300
Concord, NH 03301
603-224-6942
http://www.newhampshirelawyerreferral.com

Small Business Development Center (SBDC) Offices
New Hampshire SBDC
Whittemore School of Business & Economics, UNH
110 McConnell Hall
Durham, NH 03824
603-862-2200
http://www.nhsbdc.org

SCORE Offices
Merrimack Valley SCORE
275 Chestnut Street
Suite 133
Manchester, NH 03101
603-666-7561
http://merrimackvalley.score.org/chapters/merrimack-valley-score

NEW JERSEY

Office of the Secretary of State
Department of State, Business Action Center
PO Box 820
Trenton, NJ 08625-0820
866-534-7789
http://www.nj.gov/njbusiness/

Department of Revenue
New Jersey Division of Taxation
Bankruptcy Section
PO Box 245
Trenton, NJ 08695-0245
609-826-4400
http://www.state.nj.us/treasury/taxation/

Department of Labor
Department of Labor and Workforce Development
1 John Fitch Plaza
13th Floor, Suite D
PO Box 110
Trenton, NJ 08625-0110
609-659-9045
http://lwd.dol.state.nj.us/labor/index.html

State CPA Association (CPA Referral)
New Jersey Society of Certified Public Accountants
425 Eagle Rock Avenue
Suite 100
Roseland, NJ 07068-1723
973-226-4494
http://www.moneymattersnj.com/findacpa/search.cfm

State Bar Association (Attorney Referral)
New Jersey State Bar Association
One Constitution Square
New Brunswick, NJ 08901-1520
732-249-5000
http://www.njsba.com

Small Business Development Center (SBDC) Offices
New Jersey SBDC
Rutgers University
1 Washington Park
Suite 360
Newark, NJ 07102
973-353-1927
http://www.njsbdc.com

SCORE Offices
Essex, Hudson/Union Counties SCORE
2 Gateway Center SBA
15th Floor
Newark, NJ 07102
973-645-3982
http://essexhudsonunioncounties.score.org/chapters/essex-hudson-and-union-counties-score

NEW MEXICO

Office of the Secretary of State
New Mexico State Capitol
325 Don Gaspar Avenue #300
Santa Fe, NM 87501
505-827-3600
http://www.sos.state.nm.us/

Department of Revenue
Corporate Income and Franchise Tax
PO Box 25127
Santa Fe, NM 87504-5127
505-827-0700
http://www.tax.newmexico.gov/Businesses/Pages/Home.aspx

Department of Labor
Department of Work Force Solutions
401 Broadway, NE
Albuquerque, NM 87102
505-841-8405
http://www.dws.state.nm.us

New Mexico Public Regulation Commission
Public Regulation Commission
1120 Paseo de Peralta
PO Box 1269
Santa Fe, NM 87501
888-427-5772
http://www.nmprc.state.nm.us/corporations/corporation-forms.html

State CPA Association (CPA Referral)
New Mexico Society of CPAs
3400 Menaul Boulevard, NE
Albuquerque, NM 87107
505-246-1699
http://www.nmscpa.org/cpa_referral_search

State Bar Association (Attorney Referral)
State Bar of New Mexico
PO Box 92860
Albuquerque, NM 87199-2860
505-797-6000
http://www.nmbar.org/findattorney/attorneyfinder.aspx

Small Business Development Center (SBDC) Offices
New Mexico SBDC
Santa Fe Community College
6401 Richards Avenue
Santa Fe, NM 87508
505-428-1362
http://www.nmsbdc.org

SCORE Offices
Albuquerque SCORE
625 Silver Avenue SW
Suite 320
Albuquerque, NM 87102
505-248-8232
http://albuquerque.score.org/chapters/albuquerque-score

NEW YORK

Office of the Secretary of State
New York Secretary of State
One Commerce Plaza
99 Washington Avenue
Albany, NY 12231-0001
518-473-2492
http://www.dos.ny.gov/corps/index.html

Department of Revenue
NYS Assessment Receivables
PO Box 4127
Binghamton, NY 13902-4127
518-485-6027
http://www.tax.ny.gov/bus/

Department of Labor
Department of Labor
State Office Building, #12
W. A. Harriman Campus
Albany, NY 12240
518-457-9000
http://www.labor.ny.gov/home/businesses.asp

State CPA Association (CPA Referral)
New York Society of CPAs
3 Park Avenue
18th Floor
New York, NY 10016-5991
212-719-8300
http://www.nysscpa.org/soundadvicea.htm

State Bar Association (Attorney Referral)
New York State Bar Association
1 Elk Street
Albany, NY 12207
518-463-3200
http://www.nysba.org/AM/Template.cfm?Section=Public_Resources&
ContentID=59721&template=/CM/ContentDisplay.cfm

Small Business Development Center (SBDC) Offices
New York State SBDC
Corporate Woods, 3rd Floor
State University of New York
Albany, NY 12246
518-443-5398
http://www.nyssbdc.org

SCORE Offices
New York City SCORE
26 Federal Plaza
New York, NY 10278
212-264-4507
http://newyorkcity.score.org/chapters/new-york-city-score

NORTH CAROLINA

Office of the Secretary of State
North Carolina Department of the Secretary of State
PO Box 29622
Raleigh, NC 27626-0622
919-807-2225
http://www.secretary.state.nc.us/corporations/thepage.aspx

Department of Revenue
North Carolina Department of Revenue
PO Box 25000
Raleigh, NC 27640-0640
877-252-3052
http://www.dor.state.nc.us/business/index.html

Department of Labor
Department of Labor
1101 Mail Service Center
Raleigh, NC 27699-1101
919-807-2796
http://www.nclabor.com

State CPA Association (CPA Referral)
North Carolina Association of Certified Public Accountants
3100 Gateway Centre Boulevard
Morrisville, NC 27560
919-469-1040
http://www.ncacpa.org/Home.aspx

State Bar Association (Attorney Referral)
North Carolina State Bar
208 Fayetteville Street
PO Box 25908
Raleigh, NC 27611-5908
919-828-4620
http://www.ncbar.com/index.asp

Small Business Development Center (SBDC) Offices
North Carolina SBTDC
5 W. Hargett Street
Suite 600
Raleigh, NC 27601
919-715-7272
http://www.sbtdc.org

SCORE Offices
Chapel Hill SCORE
104 S. Estes Drive
Chapel Hill—Carrboro Chamber of Commerce
Chapel Hill, NC 27514
919-968-6894
http://chapelhill.score.org/chapters/chapel-hill-score

NORTH DAKOTA

Office of the Secretary of State
Secretary of State of North Dakota
600 E. Boulevard Avenue
Department 108, 1st Floor
Bismarck ND 58505-0500
701-328-2900
http://www.nd.gov/sos/businessserv/

Department of Revenue
North Dakota Department of Revenue
600 E. Boulevard Avenue
Bismarck, ND 58505-0599
701-328-7088
http://www.nd.gov/tax/

Department of Labor
Department of Labor
State Capitol Building
600 E. Boulevard Avenue
Department 406
Bismarck, ND 58505-0340
701-328-2660
http://www.nd.gov/labor/

State CPA Association (CPA Referral)
North Dakota CPA Society
2701 S. Columbia Road
Grand Forks, ND 58201
701-775-7100
http://www.ndscpa.org/forthepublic.htm
mail@ndscpa.org

State Bar Association (Attorney Referral)
State Bar Association of North Dakota
504 N. Washington Street
Bismarck, ND 58501
701-255-1404
https://www.sband.org/LRS/default.aspx

Small Business Development Center (SBDC) Offices
North Dakota SBDC
UND SBDC Lead Center
1200 Memorial Highway
PO Box 5509
Bismarck, ND 58506
701-328-5375
http://www.ndsbdc.org

SCORE Offices
Bismarck-Mandan SCORE
700 E. Main Avenue
2nd Floor
Bismarck, ND 58506
701-328-5861
http://bismarckmandan.score.org/chapters/bismarck-mandan-score

OHIO

Office of the Secretary of State
Ohio Secretary of State
180 E. Broad Street
16th Floor
Columbus, OH 43215
614-466-2655
http://www.sos.state.oh.us/SOS/Businesses.aspx

Department of Revenue
Ohio Department of Taxation
PO Box 530
Columbus, OH 43216-0530
888-405-4039
http://tax.ohio.gov/channels/other/business.stm

Department of Labor
Department of Commerce
77 S. High Street
23rd Floor
Columbus, OH 43215-6123
614-466-3636
http://www.com.state.oh.us

State CPA Association (CPA Referral)
Ohio Society of CPAs
535 Metro Place South
Dublin, OH 43017
888-959-1212
http://www.ohioscpa.com/financial-fitness-ohio/find-a-cpa

State Bar Association (Attorney Referral)
Ohio State Bar Association
1700 Lake Shore Drive
Columbus, OH 43204
800-282-6556
https://www.ohiobar.org/ForPublic/Pages/ForPublic.aspx

Small Business Development Center (SBDC) Offices
Ohio SBDC
77 S. High Street
28th Floor
Columbus, OH 43216
614-466-2711
http://www.entrepreneurohio.org

SCORE Offices
Columbus SCORE
401 N. Front Street
Suite 200
Columbus, OH 43215
614-469-2357
http://columbusoh.score.org/chapters/columbus-score

OKLAHOMA

Office of the Secretary of State
Secretary of State
2300 N. Lincoln Boulevard
Suite 101
Oklahoma City, OK 73105-4897
405-521-3912
https://www.sos.ok.gov/business/default.aspx

Department of Revenue
Oklahoma Tax Commission
PO Box 26890
Oklahoma City, OK 73126-0890
405-521-3160
http://www.oktax.state.ok.us/bustax.html

Department of Labor
Department of Labor
3017 N. Stiles Avenue
Suite 100
Oklahoma City, OK 73105-5212
405-521-6100
http://www.ok.gov/odol/

State CPA Association (CPA Referral)
Oklahoma Society of CPAs
1900 NW Expressway
Suite 910
Oklahoma City, OK 73118-1898
405-841-3800
http://www.oscpa.com/?316

State Bar Association (Attorney Referral)
Oklahoma Bar Association
PO Box 53036
1901 N. Lincoln Boulevard
Oklahoma City, OK 73152-3036
405-416-7000
http://www.oklahomafindalawyer.com/FindALawyer

Small Business Development Center (SBDC) Offices
Oklahoma SBDC State Office
Southeastern Oklahoma State University
1405 N. 4th Avenue
PMB 2584
Durant, OK 74701
580-745-2955
http://www.osbdc.org

SCORE Offices
Oklahoma City SCORE
301 N. 6th Street SBA
Suite 116
Oklahoma City, OK 73102
405-609-8004
http://www.osbdc.org

OREGON

Office of the Secretary of State
Oregon Secretary of State
Public Service Building
255 Capitol Street, NE
Suite 151
Salem, OR 97310-1327
503-986-2200
http://www.filinginoregon.com
corporation.division@state.or.us

Department of Revenue
Oregon Department of Revenue
955 Center Street NE
Salem, OR 97301-2555
503-378-4988
http://www.oregon.gov/dor/bus/pages/index.aspx
questions.dor@state.or.us

Department of Labor
Bureau of Labor and Industries
800 NE Oregon Street, #1045
Portland, OR 97232
http://www.oregon.gov/BOLI/
971-673-0761

State CPA Association (CPA Referral)
Oregon Society of Certified Public Accountants
10206 SW Laurel Street
Beaverton, OR 97005-3209
503-641-7200
https://secure.orcpa.org/public/find_a_cpa

State Bar Association (Attorney Referral)
Oregon State Bar
PO Box 231935
Tigard, OR 97281-1935
503-620-0222
http://www.osbar.org/public/

Small Business Development Center (SBDC) Offices
Oregon SBDC
Lane Community College
99 W. Tenth Avenue
Suite 390
Eugene, OR 97401
541-463-5250
http://www.bizcenter.org

SCORE Offices
Portland SCORE
601 SW Second Avenue
ODS Tower, Suite 950
Portland, OR 97204
503-326-3441
http://portlandor.score.org/chapters/portland-score

PENNSYLVANIA

Office of the Secretary of State
Pennsylvania Secretary of State
401 North Street
Room 206
Harrisburg, PA 17120
717-787-1057
http://www.dos.state.pa.us/portal/server.pt/community/corporations
/12457

Department of Revenue
Department of Revenue
110 N. 8th Street
Suite 204A
Philadelphia, PA 19107-2412
215-560-2056
http://www.revenue.state.pa.us/portal/server.pt/community/businesses
/11406

Department of Labor
Department of Labor and Industry
1700 Labor and Industry Building
7th and Forster Streets
Harrisburg, PA 17120
717-787-5279
http://www.dli.state.pa.us/portal/server.pt/community/l_i_home/5278

State CPA Association (CPA Referral)
Pennsylvania Institute of CPAs
Ten Penn Center
1801 Market Street
Suite 2400
Philadelphia, PA 19103
215-496-9272
http://www.picpa.org/public/referral/findcpa.aspx

State Bar Association (Attorney Referral)
Pennsylvania Bar Association
100 South Street
Harrisburg, PA 17101
http://www.pabar.org/index.asp

Small Business Development Center (SBDC) Offices
Pennsylvania SBDC
3819-33 Chestnut Street
Suite 325
Philadelphia, PA 19104
215-898-1219
http://www.pasbdc.org

SCORE Offices
Philadelphia SCORE
105 N. 22nd Street
Philadelphia, PA 19103
215-231-9880
http://philadelphia.score.org/chapters/philadelphia-score

RHODE ISLAND

Office of the Secretary of State
Rhode Island Secretary of State
148 W. River Street
Providence, RI 02904-2615
401-222-3040
http://sos.ri.gov/business/

Department of Revenue
Rhode Island Division of Taxation
One Capitol Hill
Providence, RI 02908
401-574-8935
http://www.tax.ri.gov/taxforms/

Department of Labor
Department of Labor and Training
1511 Pontiac Avenue
Cranston, RI 02920
401-462-8000
http://www.dlt.state.ri.us

State CPA Association (CPA Referral)
Rhode Island Society of CPAs
45 Royal Little Drive
Providence, RI 02904
401-331-5720
http://www.riscpa.org/find-a-cpa

State Bar Association (Attorney Referral)
Rhode Island Bar Association
115 Cedar Street
Providence, RI 02903
401-421-5740
https://www.ribar.com/LRS/Referral.aspx

Small Business Development Center (SBDC) Offices
Rhode Island SBDC
Johnson & Wales University
270 Weybosset Street
Providence, RI 02903
401-598-2706
http://www.risbdc.org

SCORE Offices
Rhode Island SCORE
380 Westminster Street
Providence, RI 02903
401-528-4561
http://ri.score.org/chapters/rhode-island

SOUTH CAROLINA

Office of the Secretary of State
Secretary of State's Office
1205 Pendleton Street
Suite 525
Columbia, SC 29201
803-734-2158
http://www.sos.sc.gov/Business_Filings

Department of Revenue
Department of Revenue
1 South Park Circle
Suite 100
Charleston, SC 29407
843-852-3600
http://www.sctax.org/default.htm

Department of Labor
Department of Labor, Licensing, & Regulations
110 Centerview Drive
Columbia, SC 29210
803-896-4300
http://www.llr.state.sc.us

State CPA Association (CPA Referral)
South Carolina Association of CPAs
570 Chris Drive
West Columbia, SC 29169
803-791-4181
http://www.scacpa.org/Content/FindaCPA.aspx

State Bar Association (Attorney Referral)
South Carolina Bar
950 Taylor Street
Columbia, SC 29201
803-799-6653
http://www.scbar.org/PublicServices/FindaLawyer/LRS.aspx

Small Business Development Center (SBDC) Offices
South Carolina SBDCs
Moore School of Business, University of South Carolina
1705 College Street
Columbia, SC 29208
803-777-3130
http://www.scsbdc.com

SCORE Offices
Midlands SCORE
1835 Assembly Street
Strom Thurmond Building, Room 1425
Columbia, SC 29201
803-765-5131
http://midlands.score.org/chapters/midlands-score

SOUTH DAKOTA

Office of the Secretary of State
South Dakota Secretary of State
State Capitol
500 E. Capitol Avenue
Pierre, SD 57501-5070
605-773-3537
http://sdsos.gov/Business/Default.aspx
openforbiz@state.sd.us

Department of Revenue
Department of Revenue
445 E. Capitol Avenue
Pierre, SD 57501-3185
605-773-3311
http://www.state.sd.us/drr2/businesstax/bustax.htm

Department of Labor
Department of Labor and Regulation
700 Governors Drive
Pierre, SD 57501-2291
605-773-3101
http://dol.sd.gov

State CPA Association (CPA Referral)
South Dakota CPA Society
1000 N. West Avenue, #100
PO Box 2080
Sioux Falls, SD 57101-1798
605-334-3848
http://www.sdcpa.org/ForthePublic/FindaCPA.aspx

State Bar Association (Attorney Referral)
State Bar of South Dakota
222 E. Capitol Avenue, #3
Pierre, SD 57501
605-224-7554
http://www.sdbar.org

Small Business Development Center (SBDC) Offices
South Dakota SBDC
University of South Dakota
414 E. Clark Street
Vermillion, SD 57069
605-677-5287
http://www.usd.edu/business/small-business-development-center/

SCORE Offices
Sioux Falls SCORE
2329 N. Career Avenue
Suite 105
Sioux Falls, SD 57107
605-330-4243
http://siouxfalls.score.org/chapters/sioux-falls-score

TENNESSEE

Office of the Secretary of State
Business Services
312 Rosa L. Parks Avenue
6th Floor, Snodgrass Tower
Nashville, TN 37243-1102
615-741-2286
http://www.tn.gov/sos/bus_svc/index.htm
business.services@tn.gov

Department of Revenue
Tennessee Department of Revenue
Andrew Jackson Building
500 Deaderick Street
Nashville, TN 37242
877-250-2299
http://www.state.tn.us/revenue/
TN.Revenue@tn.gov

Department of Labor
Department of Labor & Workforce Development
220 French Landing Drive
Nashville, TN 37243
615-741-6642
http://www.state.tn.us/labor-wfd/

State CPA Association (CPA Referral)
Tennessee Society of CPAs
201 Powell Place
Brentwood, TN 37027
615-377-3825
http://www.tscpa.com/public/referral/findcpa.aspx

State Bar Association (Attorney Referral)
Tennessee Bar Association
221 4th Avenue N
Suite 400
Nashville, TN 37219
615-383-7421
http://www.tba.org/info/find-an-attorney
email@tnbar.org

Small Business Development Center (SBDC) Offices
Middle Tennessee State University SBDC
MTSU Box 98
Murfreesboro, TN 37132
615-849-9999
http://www.tsbdc.org

SCORE Offices
Nashville SCORE
50 Vantage Way
Suite 201
Nashville, TN 37228
615-736-7621
http://nashville.score.org/chapters/nashville-score

TEXAS

Office of the Secretary of State
Corporations Section
Secretary of State
PO Box 13697
Austin, TX 78711-3697
512-463-5555
http://www.sos.state.tx.us/corp/index.shtml

Department of Revenue
Taxpayer Services and Collections
Central Services Building
1711 San Jacinto Boulevard
Suite 180
Austin, TX 78701-1416
512-463-4865
http://www.window.state.tx.us/taxes/

Department of Labor
Texas Workforce Commission
101 E. 15th Street
Austin, TX 78778-0001
512-475-2670
http://www.twc.state.tx.us

State CPA Association (CPA Referral)

Texas Society of CPAs
14651 Dallas Parkway
Suite 700
Dallas, TX 75254
972-687-8500
https://www.tscpa.org/eweb/

State Bar Association (Attorney Referral)

State Bar of Texas
Corporate Department
PO Box 12487
Austin, TX 78711
512-427-1463
http://www.texasbar.com/am/template.cfm?section=simple_search

Small Business Development Center (SBDC) Offices

North Texas SBDC
Bill J. Priest Institute of El Centro College
1402 Corinth Street
Suite 2111
Dallas, TX 75215
214-860-5831
http://www.ntsbdc.org

SCORE Offices

Austin SCORE
5524 Bee Cave Road
Westland Park, Building M, #100
Austin, TX 78746
512-928-2425
http://austin.score.org/chapters/austin-score

UTAH

Office of the Secretary of State
Division of Corporations
160 E. 300 S
2nd Floor
Salt Lake City, UT 84111
801-530-4849
http://www.utah.gov/business/

Department of Revenue
Utah State Tax Commission
210 North 1950
West Salt Lake City, UT 84134
801-297-2200
http://tax.utah.gov/business/information

Department of Labor
Utah Labor Commission
160 E. 300 S
Suite 300
Salt Lake City, UT 84111-6610
801-530-6800
http://www.laborcommission.utah.gov

State CPA Association (CPA Referral)
Utah Association of CPAs
220 E. Morris Avenue
Suite 320
Salt Lake City, UT 84115
801-466-8022
http://www.uacpa.org/public/referral/findcpa.aspx

State Bar Association (Attorney Referral)
Utah State Bar
645 S. 200 E
Salt Lake City, UT 84111
801-531-9077
http://www.utahbar.org/public/lawyer_referral_service_main.html

Small Business Development Center (SBDC) Offices
Utah Lead Center SBDC—Administration
Salt Lake Community College
9750 S. 300 West—LHM
Sandy, UT 84070
801-957-5384
http://www.utahsbdc.org

SCORE Offices
Salt Lake SCORE
310 S. Main Street
North Mezzanine
Salt Lake City, UT 84101
801-746-2269
http://saltlake.score.org/chapters/salt-lake-score

VERMONT

Office of the Secretary of State
Vermont Secretary of State
128 State Street
Montpelier VT 05633-1104
802-828-2386
http://corps.sec.state.vt.us

Department of Revenue
Vermont Department of Taxes
133 State Street
Montpelier, VT 05633
802-828-2551
http://www.state.vt.us/tax/business.shtml
taxforms@state.vt.us

Department of Labor
Department of Labor
5 Green Mountain Drive
PO Box 488
Montpelier, VT 05601-0488
802-828-4000
http://www.labor.vermont.gov

State CPA Association (CPA Referral)
Vermont Society of CPAs
100 State Street
Suite 500
Montpelier, VT 05602
802-229-4939
http://www.vtcpa.org/find_a_cpa/

State Bar Association (Attorney Referral)
Vermont Bar Association
PO Box 100
Montpelier, VT 05601-0100
802-223-2020
https://www.vtbar.org/FOR%20THE%20PUBLIC/Find%20a%20
Lawyer/Lawyer%20Referral%20Service%20Information.aspx

Small Business Development Center (SBDC) Offices
Vermont SBDC
Vermont Technical College
1 Main Street
PO Box 188
Randolph Center, VT 05061
802-728-9101
http://www.vtsbdc.org

SCORE Offices
Montpelier SCORE
87 State Street
Montpelier, VT 05601
802-828-4422
http://montpelier.score.org/chapters/montpelier-score

VIRGINIA

State Corporation Commission
State Corporation Commission (Specific Division)
PO Box 1197
Richmond, VA 23218
804-371-9967
http://www.scc.virginia.gov/clk/begin.aspx

Department of Revenue
Virginia Department of Taxation
1957 Westmoreland Street
Richmond, VA 23230
804-367-8031
http://www.tax.virginia.gov/site.cfm?alias=BusinessHome

Department of Labor
Department of Labor and Industry
Powers-Taylor Building
13 S. 13th Street
Richmond, VA 23219
804-371-2327
http://www.doli.virginia.gov

State CPA Association (CPA Referral)
Virginia Society of CPAs
4309 Cox Road
Glen Allen, VA 23060
804-270-5344
http://www.vscpa.com/public/referral/findcpa.aspx
vscpa@vscpa.com

State Bar Association (Attorney Referral)
Virginia Bar Association
Eighth & Main Building
707 E. Main Street
Suite 1500
Richmond, VA 23219-2800
804-775-0500
http://www.vsb.org/vlrs/

Small Business Development Center (SBDC) Offices
Virginia SBDC
Mason Enterprise Center—George Mason University
4031 University Drive
Suite 200
Fairfax, VA 22030
703-277-7727
http://www.virginiasbdc.org

SCORE Offices
Richmond SCORE
400 N. 8th Street
Federal Building
Richmond, VA 23219
804-771-2400
http://richmond.score.org/chapters/richmond-score

WASHINGTON

Office of the Secretary of State
Washington Secretary of State—Corporations Division
PO Box 40234
Olympia, WA 98504-0234
360-725-0377
http://www.sos.wa.gov/corps/
corps@sos.wa.gov

Department of Revenue
2101 4th Avenue
Suite 1400
Seattle, WA 98121-2300
206-727-5300
http://dor.wa.gov/content/doingbusiness/

Department of Labor
Washington Department of Labor and Industries
PO Box 44000
Olympia, WA 98504-4000
360-902-5800
http://www.lni.wa.gov

State CPA Association (CPA Referral)
Washington Society of CPAs
902 140th Ave NE
Bellevue, WA 98005-3480
425-644-4800
http://www.wscpa.org/public/referral/findcpa.aspx

State Bar Association (Attorney Referral)
Washington State Bar Association
1325 Fourth Avenue
Suite 600
Seattle, WA 98101-2539
206-443-9722
http://www.mywsba.org/Default.aspx?tabid=177

Small Business Development Center (SBDC) Offices
Washington SBDC Lead Center
Washington State University
1235 N. Post Street
Suite 201
Spokane, WA 99201
509-358-7767
http://www.wsbdc.org

SCORE Offices
Greater Seattle SCORE
2401 4th Avenue
Suite 450
Seattle, WA 98121
206-553-7320
http://seattle.score.org/chapters/greater-seattle-score

WEST VIRGINIA

Office of the Secretary of State
Secretary of State
1900 Kanawha Boulevard E
Building 1, Suite 157-K
Charleston, WV 25305
304-558-8000
http://www.sos.wv.gov/business-licensing/Pages/default.aspx

Department of Revenue
West Virginia State Tax Department
Taxpayer Services Division
PO Box 3784
Charleston, WV 25337-3784
304-558-3333
https://www.business4wv.com/b4wvpublic/default.aspx
http://www.wva.state.wv.us/wvtax/default.aspx
Business.4.WV@wv.gov

Department of Labor
West Virginia Division of Labor
State Capitol Complex, #749-B
Building #6
1900 Kanawha Boulevard E
Charleston, WV 25305
304-558-7890
http://www.wvlabor.com/newwebsite/pages/index.html

State CPA Association (CPA Referral)
West Virginia Society of CPAs
900 Lee Street East
Suite 1201
Charleston, WV 25301
304-342-5461
https://secure.wvscpa.org/resources/find_a_cpa

State Bar Association (Mediator Search Only)
West Virginia State Bar
2000 Deitrick Boulevard
Charleston, WV 25311-1231
304-558-2456
http://www.wvbar.org/default.aspx

Small Business Development Center (SBDC) Offices
West Virginia SBDC
State Capitol Complex
Building 6, Room 652
900 Kanawha Boulevard
Charleston, WV 25305
304-957-2087
http://wvsbdc.wvcommerce.org/(S(3ojwjf55hno0liz14vckgk55
))/default.aspx

SCORE Offices
Charleston SCORE
1116 Smith Street
Charleston, WV 25301
304-347-5463
http://charleston.score.org/chapters/charleston-score

WISCONSIN

Department of Financial Institutions
Wisconsin Department of Financial Institutions
345 W Washington Ave
Madison, WI 53703
608-261-9555
http://www.wdfi.org/corporations/

Department of Revenue
Wisconsin Department of Revenue
2135 Rimrock Road
Madison, WI 53713
608-266-2772
http://www.revenue.wi.gov/businesses/index.html

Department of Labor
Wisconsin Department of Workforce Development
201 E. Washington Avenue, #A400
Madison, WI 53707
608-232-0824
http://dwd.wisconsin.gov/dwd/default_business.htm

State CPA Association (CPA Referral)
Wisconsin Institute of CPAs
235 N. Executive Drive
Suite 200
Brookfield, WI 53005
262-785-0445
http://www.wicpa.org/public/referral/findcpa.aspx

State Bar Association (Attorney Referral)
State Bar of Wisconsin
PO Box 7158
Madison, WI 53707-7158
800-728-7788
http://www.legalexplorer.com/lawyer/lawyer-talk.asp

Small Business Development Center (SBDC) Offices
Wisconsin SBDC
University of Wisconsin
432 N. Lake Street
Room 423
Madison, WI 53706
608-263-7812
http://www.wisconsinsbdc.org/sbdc.htm

SCORE Offices
Madison SCORE
505 S. Rosa Road MG&E Innovation Center
Suite 37
Madison, WI 53719
608-441-2820
http://madison.score.org/chapters/madison-score

WYOMING

Office of the Secretary of State
Secretary of State
200 W. 24th Street
State Capitol Building, Room 110
Cheyenne, WY 82002-0020
307-777-7311
http://soswy.state.wy.us/Business/Business.aspx
business@wyo.gov

Department of Revenue
Department of Revenue
Herschler Building
2nd Floor W
Cheyenne, WY 82002-0110
307-777-7961
http://revenue.wyo.gov/
directorofrevenue@wyo.gov

Department of Labor
Administration and Support Division
Wyoming Department of Employment
1510 E. Pershing Boulevard
Cheyenne, WY 82002
307-777-8728
http://www.wyomingworkforce.org/Pages/default.aspx

State CPA Association (CPA Referral)
Wyoming Department of CPAs
504 W. 17th Street
Suite 200
Cheyenne, WY 82001
307-634-7039
https://www.wyocpa.org/find_a_cpa
admin@wyocpa.org

State Bar Association (Attorney Referral)
Wyoming State Bar
4124 Laramie Street
PO Box 109
Cheyenne, WY 82003
307-632-9061
http://www.wyomingbar.org

Small Business Development Center (SBDC) Offices
Wyoming SBDC State Office
University of Wyoming
1000 E. University Avenue
Department 3922
Laramie, WY 82071
307-766-3405
http://www.uwyo.edu/sbdc/

SCORE Offices
Cheyenne SCORE
1651 Carey Avenue
Suite 20
Cheyenne, WY 82001
307-632-1588
http://cheyenne.score.org/chapters/cheyenne-score

DISTRICT OF COLUMBIA

Department of Consumer and Regulatory Affairs
Department of Consumer and Regulatory Affairs
Business Registration
1100 4th Street SW
Washington, DC 20024
202-442-4400
http://dcra.dc.gov/DC/DCRA
dcra@dc.gov

Department of Revenue
Office of Tax & Revenue
Office of the Chief Financial Officer
1101 4th Street, SW
Suite W270
Washington, DC 20024
202-727-4829
http://otr.cfo.dc.gov/otr/site/default.asp

Department of Labor
Department of Employment Services
4805 Minnesota Avenue, NE
Washington, DC 20019
202-724-7000
http://www.does.dc.gov/does/site/default.asp

State CPA Association (CPA Referral)
Greater Washington Society of CPAs
1111 19th Street, NW, #1200
Washington, DC 20036
202-464-6001
http://www.gwscpa.org/find_a_cpa/
info@gwscpa.org

State Bar Association (Attorney Referral)
Bar Association of the District of Columbia
1016 16th Street, NW
Washington, DC 20036
202-223-6600
http://www.badc.org/i4a/pages/index.cfm?pageid=3325
info@badc.org

Small Business Development Center (SBDC) Offices
District of Columbia SBDC
Howard University School of Business
2600 6th Street, NW, Room 128
Washington, DC 20059
202-806-1550
http://www.dcsbdc.org

SCORE Offices
Washington DC SCORE
740 15th Street, NW
American Bar Association Building
Washington, DC 20005
202-272-0390
http://washingtondc.score.org/chapters/washington-dc-score-0

Appendix A: Guide to Small Business Administration Publications

The U.S. Small Business Administration produces a wide range of publications that break down the individual areas of knowledge that businesspeople need to have. All are available for download online at http://archive.sba.gov/tools/resourcelibrary/publications/index.html.

Here are the titles and publication numbers within the SBA collection:

Small Business Management Series

Management and Planning Series

- PROBLEMS IN MANAGING A FAMILY-OWNED BUSINESS (MP-3): Specific problems exist when attempting to make a family-owned business successful. This publication offers suggestions on how to overcome these difficulties.
- BUSINESS PLAN FOR SMALL MANUFACTURERS (MP-4): Designed to help owner-managers of a small manufacturing firm, this publication covers all the basic information necessary to develop an effective business plan.
- BUSINESS PLAN FOR SMALL CONSTRUCTION FIRMS (MP-5): This publication is designed to help an owner-managers of a small construction company pull together the resources to develop a business plan.
- PLANNING AND GOAL SETTING FOR SMALL BUSINESS (MP-6): Learn proven management techniques to help you plan for success.
- BUSINESS PLAN FOR THE SMALL RETAILER (MP-9): Business plans are essential road maps for success. Learn how to develop a business plan for a retail business.
- BUSINESS PLAN FOR SMALL SERVICE FIRMS (MP-11): Outlines the key points to be included in the business plan of a small service firm.
- CHECK-LIST FOR GOING INTO BUSINESS (MP-12): This is a must if you're thinking about starting a business. It highlights the important factors you should know in reaching a decision to start your own business.
- COMPUTERIZING YOUR BUSINESS (MP-14): Helps you forecast your computer needs, evaluate the alternatives, and select the right computer system for your business.
- BUSINESS PLAN FOR HOME-BASED BUSINESS (MP-15): Provides a comprehensive approach to developing a business plan for a home-based business.

- INSURANCE OPTIONS FOR BUSINESS CONTINUATION PLANNING (MP-20): This publication discusses the life insurance needs of small business owners and how important business life insurance is when planning for the future of business.
- INTRODUCTION TO STRATEGIC PLANNING (MP-21): This best seller helps you develop a strategic action plan for your small business.
- INVENTORY MANAGEMENT (MP-22): Discusses the purpose of inventory management, types of inventories, record keeping, and forecasting inventory levels.
- SELECTING THE LEGAL STRUCTURE FOR YOUR BUSINESS (MP-25): Discusses the various legal structures that a small business can use in setting up operations. It identifies types of legal structures and the advantages and disadvantages of each.
- EVALUATING FRANCHISE OPPORTUNITIES (MP-26): Evaluate franchise opportunities and select the business that's right for you.
- SMALL BUSINESS INSURANCE & RISK MANAGEMENT GUIDE (MP-28): This guide can help you strengthen your insurance program by identifying, minimizing, and eliminating business risks.
- HOW TO START A QUALITY CHILD CARE BUSINESS: This comprehensive manual developed by child-care professionals in both the private and public sectors, explains the business and academic dimensions of operating a child-care center.
- CHILD DAY-CARE SERVICES (MP-30): An overview of the industry, including models of day-care operations.
- HANDBOOK FOR SMALL BUSINESS (MP-31): Handy information for getting started, in a new publication developed by the SBA's Service Corps of Retired Executives (SCORE).
- HOW TO WRITE A BUSINESS PLAN (MP-32): What you need to know to write a good plan at the start. It can save your business down the line.

Financial Management Series
- ABC's OF BORROWING (FM-1): This volume tells you what lenders look for and what to expect when borrowing money for your small business.
- UNDERSTANDING CASH FLOW (FM-4): This publication shows owner-managers how to plan for the movement of cash through the business and thus plan for future requirements.

- A VENTURE CAPITAL PRIMER FOR SMALL BUSINESS (FM-5): Learn what venture capital resources are available and how to develop a proposal for obtaining these funds.
- BUDGETING IN A SMALL SERVICE FIRM (FM-8): Learn how to set up and keep sound financial records. Study how to effectively use journals, ledgers, and charts to increase profits.
- RECORDKEEPING IN A SMALL BUSINESS (FM-10): Need some basic advice on setting up a useful record keeping system? This publication describes how you can do so.
- PRICING YOUR PRODUCTS AND SERVICES PROFITABLY (FM-13): Discusses how to price your products profitably, plus various pricing techniques and when to use them.
- FINANCING FOR SMALL BUSINESS (FM-14): Learn how, when, and where to find capital for business needs, including step-by-step instructions.

Marketing Series
- CREATIVE SELLING: THE COMPETITIVE EDGE (MT-1): Explains how to use creative selling techniques to increase profits.
- MARKETING FOR SMALL BUSINESS: AN OVERVIEW (MT-2): Provides an overview of marketing concepts and contains an extensive bibliography of sources covering the subject of marketing.
- RESEARCHING YOUR MARKET (MT-8): Learn inexpensive techniques that you can apply to gather facts about your customer base and how to expand it.
- SELLING BY MAIL ORDER (MT-9): Provides basic information on how to run a successful mail-order business, including information on product selection, pricing testing, and writing effective advertisements.
- ADVERTISING (MT-11): Advertising is critical to the success of any small business. Learn how you can effectively advertise your products and services.
- SIGNS: SHOWCASING YOUR BUSINESS ON THE STREET (MT-12): For most businesses, good signage is the most economical and efficient form of attracting customers.

Product and Invention Series
- IDEAS INTO DOLLARS (PI-1): This publication identifies the main challenges in product development and provides a list of resources to

help inventors and innovators take their ideas into the marketplace.

- AVOIDING PATENT, TRADEMARK AND COPYRIGHT PROBLEMS (PI-2): Learn how to avoid infringing the rights of others and the importance of protecting your own rights.
- TRADEMARKS AND BUSINESS GOODWILL (PI-3): Learn what trademarks are and are not, and how to get the most protection for your commercial name.

Personnel Management Series

- EMPLOYEES: HOW TO FIND AND PAY THEM (PM-2): A business is only as good as the people in it. Learn how to find and hire the right employees.
- MANAGING EMPLOYEE BENEFITS (PM-3): Describes employee benefits as one part of a total compensation package and discusses the proper management of benefits.

Crime Prevention

- CURTAILING CRIME—INSIDE AND OUT (CP-2) Includes measure to safeguard against employee dishonesty, shoplifting, bad-check passing, burglary, and robbery.

Appendix B: State Tax Rates

All numbers in percentages as of 1/1/2012

State	Sales Tax*	Corporate Tax	Individual Income Tax
Alabama	4.0	6.5	2.0–5.0
Alaska	None	1.0–9.4	None
Arizona	6.6	6.968	2.59–4.54
Arkansas	6.0	1.0–6.5	1.0–7.0
California	7.25	8.84	1.0–9.3
Colorado	2.9	4.63	4.63
Connecticut	6.35	7.25	3.0–6.7
Delaware	None	8.7	2.2–6.75
Florida	6.0	5.5	None
Georgia	4.0	6.0	1.0–6.0
Hawaii	4.0	4.4–6.4	1.4–11.0
Idaho	6.0	7.6	1.6–7.8
Illinois	6.25	9.5	5.0
Indiana	7.0	8.5	3.4
Iowa	6.0	6.0–12.0	0.36–8.98
Kansas	6.3	4.0	3.5–6.45
Kentucky	6.0	4.0–6.0	2.0–6.0
Louisiana	4.0	4.0–8.0	2.0–6.0
Maine	5.0	3.5–8.93	2.0–8.5
Maryland	6.0	8.25	2.0–5.5
Massachusetts	6.25	8.0	5.3
Michigan	6.0	6.0	4.35
Minnesota	6.875	9.8	5.35–7.85
Mississippi	7.0	3.0–5.0	3.0–5.0
Missouri	4.225	6.25	1.5–6.0
Montana	None	6.75	1.0–6.9
Nebraska	5.5	5.58–7.81	2.56–6.84
Nevada	6.85	None	None
New Hampshire	None	8.5	5.0 on dividends/interest income only

State	Sales Tax*	Corporate Tax	Individual Income Tax
New Jersey	7.0	9.0	1.4–8.97
New Mexico	5.125	4.8–7.6	1.7–4.9
New York	4.0	7.1	4.0–8.82
North Carolina	4.75	6.9	6.0–7.75
North Dakota	5.0	1.7–5.2	1.51–3.99
Ohio	5.5	**	0.587–5.925
Oklahoma	4.5	6.0	0.5–5.25
Oregon	None	6.6–7.6	5.0–9.9
Pennsylvania	6.0	9.99	3.07
Rhode Island	7.0	9.0	3.75–5.99
South Carolina	6.0	5.0	0–7.0
South Dakota	4.0	None	None
Tennessee	7.0	6.5	6.0 on dividends/ interest income only
Texas	6.25	***	None
Utah	5.95	5.0	5.0
Vermont	6.0	6.0–8.5	3.55–8.95
Virginia	5.0	6.0	2–5.75
Washington	6.5	None	None
West Virginia	6.0	7.5	3.0–6.5
Wisconsin	5.0	7.9	4.6–7.75
Wyoming	4.0	None	None
District of Columbia	6.0	9.975	4.0–8.95

Source: Federation of Tax Administrators

*Includes exemptions for food and drugs; doesn't include additional local taxes

**Ohio doesn't have a standard corporate tax; it charges commercial and franchise taxes instead.

***Texas imposes a franchise tax, otherwise known as a margin tax.

Appendix C: Worksheets

Is Being in Business for You?

Not everyone's ready for the reality of business. Consider the following before you make the commitment to starting your own company:

Question	Yes	/ No
1. Are you an organizer? A self-starter?	❑	❑
2. Can you tolerate a variety of personalities?	❑	❑
3. Can you make solid decisions quickly?	❑	❑
4. Is your health good?	❑	❑
5. Do you understand business finance?	❑	❑
6. Can you work 10-12 hour days, with no weekends?	❑	❑
7. Have you talked with your family about business goals?	❑	❑
8. Do you have a business plan?	❑	❑
9. Will you have to borrow money?	❑	❑
10. Are your family finances in good shape?	❑	❑
11. Do you really believe in your ideas	❑	❑
12. Have you ever hired anyone before?	❑	❑
13. Have you ever talked to anyone in this industry before?	❑	❑
14. Have you thought about where you'll locate the business?	❑	❑
15. Do you understand social media and communicating online?	❑	❑

Planning the Business Plan: An Outline

A business plan is a make-or-break document with lenders; investors; and, in certain cases, potential customers for a new business. Here's a handy form to help you organize the information you'll need in your business plan:

Executive Summary: This section kicks off the plan, but you should write it at the end after you've had the chance to create the rest of the document. An executive summary should be no longer than one page and should encapsulate the business, its products and services, risks, opportunities target strategies, competition, finances, and your projected return on investment.

_____

_____

_____

Mission Statement: A one- or two-sentence statement that describes the culture of your business and its goals.

_____
_____
_____
_____
_____
_____
_____
_____
_____

Business Concept: Explains what the business is you want to finance; the technology, concept, or strategy on which it is based; and its short-term business objectives.

_____
_____
_____
_____
_____
_____
_____
_____
_____

Management Team: Lists the chief executive officer and key management figures by name, along with their experience, past successes, and achievements that might attract lenders, investors, and customers.

_____
_____
_____
_____
_____
_____
_____
_____
_____

Industry Analysis: This section gives an informed overview of market share, leadership, players, market shifts, costs, pricing, and competition that provide the opportunity for the new company's success.

_____

_____

_____

_____

_____

_____

_____

_____

Financial Analysis: This section outlines the complete financial state of the business thus far. It indicates in detail your current financial state, future financial goals, and your current capital requirements and start-up costs. Depending on your industry, you may be doing a one-to three-year projection on costs, projected revenue, and anticipated profitability.

_____

_____

_____

_____

_____

_____

_____

_____

Day-to-Day Operations: Describes staffing plans, training, and other personnel-related issues. How will you use people? This section also talks about business support activities such as advertising and marketing.

_____

_____

_____

_____

_____

_____

_____

_____

Financing Needs: This is the detailed section that explains what you have to invest and what you'll need from lenders. Most important, in this section explain how long you expect to pay back any financing.

_____

_____

_____

_____

_____

_____

_____

Summary: As appropriate, a one-page narrative or set of bullets summarizing what you've just told readers.

_____

_____

_____

_____

_____

_____

_____

_____

_____

_____

Appendix: Lenders want to see tax returns and any other third-party information that will help them know about the business.

_____

_____

_____

_____

_____

_____

_____

Questions and Answers Worksheet

Use this worksheet to jot down questions you have about the process of starting a business. The sources provided in this book should help you answer almost any question you come up with.

Q. _____

_____

_____

A. _____

_____

_____

_____

Q. _____

_____

A. _____

_____

_____

_____

Q. _____

_____

A. _____

_____

_____

_____

Q. _____

_____

A. _____

_____

_____

_____

_____

The Nine Great Steps Checklist

Write down the date that you complete each step.

❑ **Step 1:** Determine Your Product or Service
Date Completed: _____

❑ **Step 2:** Research Your Idea
Date Completed: _____

❑ **Step 3:** Make the Internet Work for You
Date Completed: _____

❑ **Step 4:** Develop a Business Plan
Date Completed: _____

❑ **Step 5:** Consult a Lawyer, an Accountant, and a Financial Planner
Date Completed: _____

❑ **Step 6:** Determine Your Business Entity
Date Completed: _____

❑ **Step 7:** Seek Government Help
Date Completed: _____

❑ **Step 8:** Start Your Business (File All Necessary Forms)
• Federal Identification Number Registration
Date Completed: _____
• State and Local Business Registration
Date Completed: _____
• State Tax Registration
Date Completed: _____

❑ **Step 9:** Seek Sources of Financing
Date Completed: _____

Notes: _____

_____

_____

Index

Notes

Notes

Notes